PSHE and

citizenship

ages 7–11

Gillian Goddard & Jacqueline Barbera

Published by Scholastic Ltd,
Villiers House,
Clarendon Avenue,
Leamington Spa,
Warwickshire
CV32 5PR
www.scholastic.co.uk

Printed by Ebenezer Baylis & Son Ltd, Worcester
Text © 2002 Gillian Goddard and Jacqueline Barbera
© 2002 Scholastic Ltd
1 2 3 4 5 6 7 8 9 0 2 3 4 5 6 7 8 9 0 1

Authors
Gillian Goddard and Jacqueline Barbera

Editor
Roanne Davis

Assistant Editor
Dulcie Booth

Series designer
Lynne Joesbury

Designers
Clare Brewer and Paul Cheshire

Illustrations
Beverly Curl

Cover illustration
Jon Berkeley

British Library Cataloguing-in-Publication Data
A catalogue record for this book is available from the British Library.

ISBN 0-439-98330-4

Designed using Adobe Pagemaker

Contents

Acknowledgements

Aladdin Books Ltd for the use of an extract from *Let's Talk About Bullying* by Angela Grunsell © 1989, Angela Grunsell (1989, Aladdin Books). **British Heart Foundation** for the use of an extract from *Hack!* text by Philip Boys © 1998, British Heart Foundation and 'The way to a healthy heart is through the stomach' from *Bodyfile* leaflet (this leaflet is out of print) © 1998, British Heart Foundation www.bhf.org.uk. **Curtis Brown Literary Agents** for the use of 'I Like to Stay Up' by Grace Nichols from *Another Second Poetry Book* edited by John Foster © 1987, Grace Nichols (1987, Oxford University). **Child's Play (International) Ltd** for the use of text and an illustration from *Bully for you* by M Twinn © 1991, M Twinn. (1991, Child's Play (International) Ltd) Swindon, UK. **Gwen Dunn** for the use of 'I went back' by Gwen Dunn from *The Livelong Day* © Gwen Dunn (BBC Radio for Schools). **Egmont Books Ltd** for the use of text from *I am David* by Anne Holm, English translation © 1965. First published as *David* by Gyldendal, Copenhagen. **Egmont Children's Books Ltd** for the use of an extract from *The Kingdom by the Sea* by Robert Westall © 1990, The Estate of Robert Westall (1990, Methuen). **Gillian Goddard** for the use of 'Fight for Blackwater' by Gillian Goddard from *Junior Focus* magazine © 1999, Gillian Goddard (1999, Scholastic Ltd); the use of 'Set a thief to catch a thief' by Gillian Goddard from *Junior Focus* magazine © Gillian Goddard (Scholastic Ltd); the use of 'Diary of Elfrith: January 7' from *History study kits: The Anglo-Saxons* © 1994, Gillian Goddard (1994, Scholastic Ltd); the use of 'Look before you leap' by Gillian Goddard from *Junior Focus* magazine © Gillian Goddard (Scholastic Ltd); the use of 'A friend in need' by Gillian Goddard from *Junior Focus* magazine © Gillian Goddard (Scholastic Limited). **HMSO** for the use of text and for basing illustrations on those in the leaflet *Get Out – Get the Brigade Out – Stay Out or how to survive a fire in your home* © 1996, Crown Copyright (May 1996, Home Office Communication Directorate Code). **David Higham Associates** for the use of an extract from *The Sword in the Stone* by TH White © TH White (Collins); the use of an extract from *The Bully* by Jan Needle © 1993, Jan Needle (1993, Hamish Hamilton); the use of 'The Jigsaw Puzzle' by Russell Hoban from *Allsorts 3* © Russell Hoban. **John Kitching** for the use of 'Beware' by John Kitching from *Another Second Poetry Book* edited by John Foster © 1998, John Kitching (1998, Oxford University Press). **Jay Landesman** for the use of 'Crying to get out' by Fran Landesman from *Golden Handshake* © 1981, Fran Landesman. **Caroline Nystrom** for the use of an extract from *Andy's Big Question* by Caroline Nystrom © 1987, Caroline Nystrom (1987, Lion Publishing); the use of an extract from *Mike's Lonely Summer* by Caroline Nystrom © 1986, Caroline Nystrom (1986, Lion Publishing); the use of an extract from *The Trouble With Josh* by Caroline Nystrom © 1989, Caroline Nystrom (1989, Lion Publishing). **Orion Publishing Ltd** for the use of an extract from *Shadow of the Minotaur* by Alan Gibbons © 2000, Alan Gibbons (2000, Orion Children's Books). **Pearson Education** for the use of an extract 'The Balaclava story' from *The Fib and other stories* by George Layton © 1975, George Layton (1975, Longman). **Penguin Books Ltd** for the use of 11 lines from 'Objection' from *Cat Among the Pigeons* by Kit Wright © 1984, 1987, Kit Wright (1987, Viking Kestrel); an extract from *Scribbleboy* by Philip Ridley © 1997, Philip Ridley (1997, Viking). **Penguin Group Books Ltd** for the use of 'The Really Ugly Duckling' from *The Stinky Cheese Man and other Fairly Stupid Tales* by Jon Scieszka and Lane Smith. Text © 1992, Jon Scieska. **The Peters Fraser and Dunlop Group** for the use of 'I know someone' and 'Tricks' from *Quick, Let's Get Out of Here* by Michael Rosen © 1983. Michael Rosen (1983, Puffin). **The Random House Group** for the use of the limericks 'A brave taxi driver called Clive' and 'A deep-water sailor called Rod' from *Limericks* by Michael Palin © Michael Palin (Red Fox) **The Society of Authors as the Literary Representative of The Estate of Alfred Noyes** for the use of an extract from 'The Highwayman' by Alfred Noyes © 1981, Alfred Noyes (1981, Oxford University Press). **Walker Books Ltd** for the use of one illustration and an extract of text from *Goodbye Max* by Holly Keller © 1987, Holly Keller (1987, Walker Books). **The Watts Publishing Group Ltd** for the use of an extract from *Let's Talk About Racism* by Angela Grunsell © 1990, Angela Grunsell (1990, Franklin Watts).

Every effort has been made to trace copyright holders and the publishers apologise for any omissions.

Introduction

The new National Curriculum (2000) included for the first time a specific personal social and health education (PSHE) with citizenship curriculum. Though non-mandatory at Key Stages 1 and 2, it is an important component of the education children receive in primary school, one for which OFSTED will be looking for evidence.

The delivery of PSHE and citizenship in primary school has always occurred to some extent, whether planned or unplanned. It is delivered through the curriculum and as an implicit part of the pastoral support and disciplinary systems in place in school. Many of the specific objectives in the PSHE and citizenship curriculum can be matched to aspects of current medium- and short-term plans, especially in the Literacy Hour, RE, science, the humanities and subjects such as PE, music and art.

The demands of the new PSHE and citizenship syllabus

The PSHE and citizenship objectives for Key Stages 1 and 2, as set out in the curriculum guidelines, cover four main sections or themes:

1. Developing confidence and responsibility and making the most of their abilities.
2. Preparing to play an active role as citizens.
3. Developing a healthy, safer lifestyle.
4. Developing good relationships and respecting the differences between people.

The first section includes work on feelings, communication and upon building self-esteem. It develops skills needed to find solutions to problems and to accept the impact of growing up. It also asks children to consider future occupations and finance management.

The next section contains a mixture of objectives centring upon the need for rules and laws, together with the identification of right and wrong and the reasons for that distinction. As the children progress through the key stage, it also demands some examination of the complexity of making moral choices. Contribution to the school, the family and the community, in local, national and global dimensions is asked for. Finding non-violent ways of resolving conflict is covered, along with aspects of democratic government, at a school, local and national and European level. Environmental issues are considered against an economic background. Finally, the media and its impact on attitudes are explored.

The third section is linked strongly with the science curriculum. It requires children to make healthier lifestyle choices, to keep safe through sensible risk assessment, management of peer pressure, drug and alcohol education and sexual abuse awareness. Puberty and its effects are also covered, but further aspects of sex education are left to the discretion of the school governors. First aid and health and safety rules are gone through.

The last section focuses upon equal opportunities issues, empathy and on the children understanding the impact of their actions, words and behaviour upon others, including bullying.

Teaching PSHE and citizenship through texts

The use of texts, particularly those that stimulate the imagination and allow rehearsal of situations in the children' minds, enables the development of specific concepts and skills. Discussion of motives and character, of prediction and the consequences of plot development, and the building up of an *emotional* vocabulary all help children to recognise feelings and dangers, say what they need clearly, be able to listen and begin to compromise, consider alternative ways of solving problems and become aware of situations and institutions that are new to them. The Literacy Strategy work also encourages children to have the confidence to speak out, to enter into collective activities and to organise and manage their own learning. It is only a short step from the current work being undertaken in the Literacy Hour, promoting high literacy standards, to using that work explicitly to develop children as individuals and members of society. It can be fun and creative too!

Achieving the PSHE and citizenship syllabus objectives through this book

Key Stage 2 teachers will soon be receiving children who have already had planned experiences to develop their awareness of PSHE and citizenship issues. Progression can be built into the planning frameworks. To aid this progression, this book is produced with a sister book for Key Stage 1. As with the infant book, this book aims to provide practical support for the class teacher by providing a bank of texts and related activities that can be incorporated into the Literacy Hour, and other cross-curricular work, to deliver the PSHE and citizenship objectives. Although the material is organised into thematic chapters – Growing up, Relationships and respecting differences, Developing self-esteem, Coping with crisis and loss, Managing conflict, Keeping safe and healthy, and Citizenship, the holistic nature of PSHE and citizenship means that these divisions can be treated as guidelines only. Certain texts will have activities that address several themes. This flexibility in use will increase the book's value as a tool for your teaching.

Each chapter contains a series of texts of differing genres, followed by ideas for discussing the text. These include reference to literacy points as well as syllabus objectives within a focused textual framework. Identification of key vocabulary is given, as well as ideas for displaying work undertaken by the children during the activities, or other display ideas to introduce or reinforce the text's main concepts. This is followed by a series of suggested PSHE and citizenship activities. Further literacy activities conclude the examination of each text, to support independent activities and guide writing tasks. The appropriate PSHE and citizenship objectives met through this work are given each time. These objectives can be achieved through completion of the activities themselves and as a product of the process of organised sharing, co-operation, discussion and research necessary for the achievement of the activities.

The stress on the development of generic skills and attitudes within the syllabus means that virtually all the texts address automatically the following objectives:
◆ To talk and write about their opinions, and explain their views, on issues that affect themselves and society (1a).
◆ To reflect on spiritual, moral, social and cultural issues, using imagination to understand other people's experiences (2e).
◆ To understand that their actions affect themselves and others, to care about other people's feelings and to try to see things from their points of view (4a).

These are to be taken as common to all tasks in addition to those named for each text and are therefore not specified each time.

The following grid summarises the themes, objectives and genre of each text. The activities are appropriate for particular year groups, though you will need to adapt the ideas to suit the particular abilities and stages of development of the children in your class. The texts have been chosen to reflect the range of interests across the key stage, so one specific text may not be suitable for all age groups.

PSHE and citizenship work offers the chance to recapture some of those enjoyable, interesting and creative dimensions in the children's work. Enjoy it.

Growing up

In this chapter, texts are used to investigate issues which arise as children grow up. During Key Stage 2, the rate at which children develop will vary. This will be linked to age, physical development, home life and personal experiences. At age 11, when they leave for secondary school, some children will still be quite immature, others very streetwise. The different texts and activity ideas in this chapter may be appropriate for different ages. For example, 'Shirley Said' is more suitable for Years 3 and 4, whereas 'The Highwayman' is better for Year 6. Other texts, for example 'The Jigsaw Puzzle', can often be used with younger children initially, but developed for more mature children.

The theme of growing up covers a whole range of issues, from physical and emotional changes to development in relationships, beginning to be attracted to the opposite sex and coping with all the embarrassing changes of puberty. Children need to be helped to realise that these embarrassing developments are natural and happen to everyone, but they also need to be aware that changes will happen at different times for each individual. As a teacher, you will need to judge which text and which activities will be appropriate for your children and decide how much information about physical changes is relevant to them. For this reason, openings are provided in the discussion ideas, but you will need to develop them for your class.

Although PSHE and citizenship includes sex education, a specific text on the physical aspect of this has not been included due to its extremely sensitive nature. However, many of the ideas in the texts develop the emotional and social side of relationships and could be easily used to lead to sex education where schools feel this would be appropriate. Remember that there has to be a school policy on sex education and parents are legally entitled to opt children out if they so wish. It is therefore important that you plan carefully the use of any text that may lead to discussion of sex education beyond that in the National Curriculum.

Genre
short
humorous
poetry

Shirley Said

Who wrote 'kick me' on my back?

Who put a spider in my mack?

Who's the one who pulls my hair?

Tries to trip me everywhere?

Who runs up to me and strikes me?

That boy there – I think he likes me.

Dennis Doyle

Shirley Said

Display the children's illustrations and descriptions of present and future relationships, and personal-space posters.

PSHE and citizenship learning objectives

◆ To recognise, as they approach puberty, how people's emotions change at that time and how to deal with their feelings towards themselves, their family and others in a positive way (1d).

◆ To be aware of different types of relationship, including marriage and those between friends and families, and to develop the skills to be effective in relationships (4c).

◆ To feel positive about themselves (5b).

Background notes

This poem illustrates how relationships are often not what they seem and that we may behave in ways that don't reflect our feelings because we don't understand them or are embarrassed by them.

Vocabulary

Relationships, family, sibling, friend, upset, emotion, embarrassed.

Discussing the text

◆ Covering up the final line and the illustration, read the poem with the children. Ask them to discuss with a partner what type of person the narrator might be. Male or female? How old? Who do they think is being talked about? A friend? A sibling? A classmate? An older child at school? Encourage the children to suggest evidence from the text to support their ideas.

◆ Share the ideas from the discussion and draw out the fact that there are a whole range of relationships this poem could be about. Scribe the ideas along with the supporting evidence from the text onto a board or flip chart.

◆ Ask the children to predict the content of the final line. Write these ideas on the board.

◆ Read the final line of the poem with the children. Who do they think is writing the poem now? Why? Discuss why it is likely to be a girl. How old do they think the girl is? Who is she asking the questions of?

PSHE and citizenship activities

◆ Re-read the final line of the poem again. Discuss how this line subtly changes the meaning of the earlier lines. Ask the children why they think the person in the poem has done all these things to someone they may 'like'. Discuss the term *like*. What does it mean in the context of this poem? Encourage the children to think of words that could be used instead of *like*. Many of these will probably be colloquial. (See links to this in the literacy ideas.) What is a girlfriend or boyfriend? Ask the children to write about someone they like in this way, without saying who it is. For anyone reluctant or feeling shy about this, it may be better to write about a good friend.

◆ With older children, develop the idea of girlfriends and boyfriends. Who has one? What makes a boy- or girlfriend different from a good friend? When they are older, what do the children think will happen to themselves in terms of relationships? Will they get married? Make the children aware of the roles of families and marriage, but be sensitive to those children who may be anti-marriage due to personal experience. Stress that marriages can be very happy if we find the right person and aren't rushed into getting married because it's expected. Ask the children to write about the partnership and family life they think they would like in the future.

◆ Ask the children to think about why the boy in the poem has been doing these 'nasty' things to the girl. Do they seem typical of things we do to people we like? Would we do them to our best friends? Have any of the children ever found themselves doing horrible things to people they really like? Why? What happened? Discuss with the children the embarrassment that can surround relationships with the opposite gender and assure them that it is normal to feel like this.

◆ Get the children to think about all the different types of relationships they have in their lives and sort them into different categories. They could choose the category headings in discussion with a partner or in a group. For example *family* – gran, granddad, mum, sister and so on; *friends* – classmates and neighbours; *other significant adults* – teacher, Brownie leader, mum's best friend.

◆ Tell the children about how their feelings and emotions will change towards different people as they grow up. Make this appropriate to the age of class you are teaching. For example, lower junior boys are probably starting to not want their mums to kiss them goodbye in front of their friends, girls may begin to be less happy sharing a bath with their brothers as they get to five or six. Ask the children to share their feelings about similar things and help them to realise that many other people will feel the same way. In small groups, ask the children to perform short improvisations around a situation which someone may feel uneasy or embarrassed about. You need to be aware of sensitive issues that could arise and, in an extreme case, may be linked to child abuse. Make sure you know what to do if a child discloses something like this to you. Check the school policy, and never take on responsibility for following up an issue on your own – seek the right support for your own and the child's sake.

◆ In discussion, help the children to realise that their physical personal space is precious and no one should encroach upon that space if they are not happy with being close to that person. Stress that it is alright to say *No* to unwanted attention and that any reasonable person would understand. Encourage the children to produce posters to show younger children when and how to say *No*.

Further literacy ideas

◆ Ask the children to use thesauruses to find verbs that have similar meanings to *like*. They should then use these sets of words to describe different relationships, for example with their parents, girlfriend or boyfriend, friend, best friend.

◆ The children could write a short poem in the style of 'Shirley Said', but a positive one about how a person contributes to their lives. For example

Who gives me a hug and shows she loves me?
Who makes my tea even when I've been bad?
Who tidies my room and, makes my bed?
That's my mum – I know she loves me.

◆ Investigate the use of question marks and open and closed questions. Can the children identify and sort types of questions? Introduce the term *rhetorical question* and encourage the children to write their own rhetorical questions.

◆ Discuss the use of standard English and dialect, linking this to the word *like*, and alternatives for it. Help the children to make a collection of words that could be used when speaking to friends but not if we were writing in standard English.

The Jigsaw Puzzle

Genre
verse poem
with an ABAB
rhyming
pattern

My beautiful picture of pirates and treasure
Is spoiled, and almost I don't want to start
To put it together; I've lost all the pleasure
I used to find in it: there's one missing part.

I know there's one missing – they lost it, the others,
The last time they played with my puzzle – and – maybe
There's more than one missing: along with the brothers
And sisters who borrow my toys there's the baby.

There's a hole in the ship or the sea that it sails on,
And I said to my father, "Well, what shall I do?
It isn't the same now that some of it's gone."
He said, "Put it together; the world's like that too."

Russell Hoban

The Jigsaw Puzzle

Display some of the children's treasured possessions, or photographs of them, and, if you still have them, some things that you used to love as a child.

PSHE and citizenship learning objective

◆ To see why and how rules and laws are made and enforced, why different rules are needed in different situations and how to take part in making and changing rules (2b).

Background notes

This is a difficult piece to read aloud because of the punctuation. Children may need help to interpret the pace and rhythm initially and reading it may need to be modelled for younger children.

Vocabulary

Punctuation, dash, colon, semicolon, comma, full stop, speech mark, question mark, apostrophe, pace, moral, treasured possession, favourite, precious, special.

Discussing the text

◆ Read the poem aloud with the children following. Encourage them to note where you pause and where the emphasis is placed, linked to the punctuation. Help the children to notice where the rhymes occur and to establish the punctuation, therefore enabling them to grasp the rhythm of the piece. Ask the children to read the poem through again with you, having heard how to read it.

◆ Go through each verse in turn, encouraging the children to explain what story the author is telling. What is the poem about? How does the child feel about the damage to his treasured toy?

◆ Discuss with the children how we all have special possessions. These are not necessarily expensive but have sentimental value to us. Talk about respecting other people's possessions and understanding that what may not seem important to them may be like the crown jewels to someone else.

◆ Help the children to make connections between the damaging of a toy and the comment made by the father in the poem. Discuss what he meant and how the feelings the child had could be transferred to all areas of life. Explore this further, encouraging children to share their experiences about times when they have been disappointed. For example, they didn't get the birthday or Christmas present they were hoping for, a friend has not turned up to play, an adult has forgotten a promise.

◆ Focus on the last verse again. What do the children think the writer's father means by *Put it together; the world's like that too*? What can we learn from this? Discuss the idea of the moral of a story. (Perhaps that life doesn't always happen as we expect it to and we have to get on and make the most of a situation.) Give an example such as when a friend won't play with someone, he or she could go and play with someone else this time, rather than sulking about it.

PSHE and citizenship activities

◆ If using this text with older children, ask them in pairs or small groups to decide how the piece should be read and rehearse a performance of it. Ask them to discuss the punctuation and, after sharing the presentations, talk about the various interpretations.

◆ Ask the children if they have a toy that had been their favourite for years and has been spoiled or damaged over time or by someone else. Tell them to write about the toy, explaining why they liked it so much, how they felt when it was damaged and how they feel about it now. Alternatively, the children could write about the favourite toy or other possession they have now and how they would feel if it were damaged.

◆ Ask the children to show their treasured possession (or photograph of it) to their partner, explaining why it is so special. Encourage them to say, for example, how long they have had it, where it came from, who gave it to them.

◆ Help the children to make up a set of rules about how to treat other people's possessions. Display these with the artefacts brought in by the children and adopt them as class rules.

◆ Ask the children to write about a time when they have been disappointed or let down by someone, or something not happening the way they expected. How did they feel? How do they think the other person felt? Talk about how to apologise and why this is necessary for other people to feel appreciated. What have they learned from this in terms of how we should behave towards other people? Encourage them to demonstrate in their writing their understanding that sometimes things happen for reasons beyond people's control.

◆ Individually, ask the children to make a list of five reasons why we should say sorry to others.

◆ Make a treasures box of your own to share with the children. The children could then make their own by bringing in a shoe box or something similar to decorate or by making one in design and technology. Ask each child to put into their personal box one special photo, a description of a special memory, a precious possession, and two other things of their choice. The boxes can then be taken home for the children to continue to use and build up as a memento of their childhood.

◆ Make a class treasures box to add to throughout the year, containing examples of the children's best work, a class's favourite story or poem, a class photograph and so on. This can be kept in school and the contents examined when the children are about to move to secondary school.

Further literacy ideas

◆ With the help of a grammar book, the children could explore the types of punctuation used in the text and learn the names and uses of each type. Then ask them to write an explanation in their own words for the use of each type. This can be used for a display in the classroom writing area.

◆ Investigate the types of sentences and phrases in the poem, looking particularly at the word order, 'incomplete' sentences and so on. Ask the children to use this style of writing to create a poem or short prose piece about something memorable that has happened to them, for example a playground incident or a day out.

The really ugly duckling

Genre
humorous,
modern,
succinct
retelling of a
traditional
story

Once upon a time there was a mother duck and a father duck who had seven baby ducklings. Six of them were regular-looking ducklings. The seventh was a really ugly duckling.

Everyone used to say, "What a nice looking bunch of ducklings – all except that one. Boy, he's really ugly."

The really ugly duckling heard these people, but he didn't care. He knew that one day he would probably grow up to be a swan and be bigger and look better than anything in the pond.

Well, as it turned out, he was just a really ugly duckling. And he grew up to be just a really ugly duck. The End.

Jon Scieszka

The really ugly duckling

Make a collection of rewritten fairy tales by Jon Scieszka and other authors, such as Roald Dahl and Tony Ross. Display them with the children's own retellings.

PSHE and citizenship learning objectives

◆ To recognise their worth as individuals by identifying positive things about themselves and their achievements, seeing their mistakes, making amends and setting personal goals (1b).

◆ To recognise, as they approach puberty, how people's emotions change at that time and how to deal with their feelings towards themselves and others in a positive way (1d).

◆ To explore how the media present information (2k).

◆ To learn about how the body changes as they approach puberty (3c).

◆ To understand that differences and similarities between people arise from a number of factors (4f).

Background notes

Many traditional tales have been retold. In this text, Jon Scieszka takes a typical traditional story and cleverly unpicks the idea of a happy ending as a traditional tale characteristic.

Vocabulary

Fairy tale, traditional, version, ugly, physical appearance, characteristics.

Discussing the text

◆ Read the story with the children all the way through. Discuss their initial reaction to the text. Were they surprised by the ending? Why? What did they think would happen at the end of the story and why? Many children will make reference to the original fairy tale here.

◆ Compare this story with the original version. What are the major differences, in both style and content? Look at the typical characteristics of a 'straight' traditional tale, for example the happy ending, and explore how they are remodelled.

◆ Discuss how the duck felt when he was young, encouraging the children to use evidence from the text to support their comments. Then ask them how they think he would feel as a grown-up.

◆ Ask the children to think about how Mum and Dad duck felt about all of their offspring and what they looked like. Do they think they would feel any different about any of them? (They would love them all equally, but may be more protective of the ugly duckling because they know he may get picked on.)

PSHE and citizenship activities

◆ Discuss with the class the beginning of the text which describes the family set-up. Ask the children to begin a story about themselves in a similar way. Advise them to write about their own family set up in the style of the text and developing the idea of something special or unusual about themselves, for example *Once upon a time there was a mother who had one little girl. She was a quiet, well-behaved little girl but she couldn't sing in tune. Everyone used to say…*

◆ Ask the children to think about how they would like to look when they grow up, and how they would like to be thought of by others. In pairs, tell them to discuss which of these aspirations are achievable and how they might develop certain characteristics, and which are unlikely and are just wishful thinking. Ask the children to set themselves a range of goals for when they are older, for example *go to college, have long hair, be a famous footballer, be a patient daughter to an elderly parent, have lots of friends, keep in touch with a best friend.*

◆ A lot of perceptions and ideas of beauty and ugliness come from media expectations. With the children's help, collect a variety of advertisements from magazines and discuss the appearances of the models. How realistic are these images for most of us? Does it matter that we don't look a certain way? Help the children to understand that what is attractive to one person may not be to another. Draw out the fact that it is our personalities and actions that matter more than our appearance. Ask for examples of how people can help others and be good citizens.

◆ Ask the children to make a list of their positive and negative characteristics. Tell them to swap these with a partner and judge if they are accurate self-perceptions. How could some of the more negative things be changed?

◆ Using non-fiction texts about growing up, ask the children to find out how their bodies will change as they reach puberty and change into adults. Help them to appreciate that these changes will be physical and emotional. Share the findings with the rest of the class and together categorise the changes into emotional and physical. It is important that children are aware that these changes will occur at different rates and at different ages for each individual. It is also important for them to understand that it is natural for them to feel uncomfortable and emotional about all these changes.

◆ Using the researched information and ideas from the class discussion, ask the children to work in groups of two or three to produce a guide to becoming a teenager. They may like to interview older children, brothers and sisters or parents to get additional ideas for this.

Further literacy ideas

◆ Investigate the styles and voices of traditional fairy tales. Collect and examine examples of story beginnings, endings, settings, character detail and so on.

◆ Look at other stories by Jon Sciesza, for example *The Frog Prince Continued* and *The True Story of the 3 Little Pigs!*, and works by other authors who have rewritten fairy tales, such as Tony Ross and Roald Dahl. Then ask the children to choose another traditional fairy story and, in pairs, work on changing it to make a humorous version. For example, a new 'Hansel and Gretel' where the witch just eats up the kids! These can be edited and published with illustrations to make a class library of alternative fairy tales.

The Highwayman

Genre
longer classic
narrative
poetry with a
lyrical
rhythm and a
rhyming
pattern

And the highwayman came riding—
      Riding— riding—
The highwayman came riding, up to the old inn-door.

He'd a French cocked-hat on his forehead, a bunch of lace at his chin,
A coat of the claret velvet, and breeches of brown doe-skin.
They fitted never with a wrinkle. His boots were up to the thigh.
And he rode with a jewelled twinkle,
      His pistol butts a-twinkle,
His rapier hilt a-twinkle, under the jewelled sky.

Over the cobbles he clattered and clashed in the dark inn-yard.
He tapped with his whip on the shutters, but all was locked and barred.
He whistled a tune to the window, and who should be waiting there
But the landlord's black-eyed daughter,
      Bess, the landlord's daughter,
Plaiting a dark red love-knot into her long black hair.

And dark in the dark old inn-yard a stable-wicket creaked
Where Tim the ostler listened. His face was white and peaked.
His eyes were hollows of madness, his hair like mouldy hay,
But he loved the landlord's daughter,
      The landlord's red-lipped daughter.
Dumb as a dog he listened, and he heard the robber say—

"One kiss, my bonny sweetheart, I'm after a prize to-night,
But I shall be back with the yellow gold before the morning light;
Yet, if they press me sharply, and harry me through the day,
Then look for me by moonlight,
      Watch for me by moonlight,
I'll come to thee by moonlight, though hell should bar the way."

He rose upright in the stirrups. He scarce could reach her hand,
But she loosened her hair i' the casement. His face burnt like a brand
As the black cascade of perfume came tumbling over his breast;
And he kissed its waves in the moonlight,
      (Oh, sweet black waves in the moonlight!)
Then he tugged at his rein in the moonlight, and galloped away to the west.

Alfred Noyes

The Highwayman

Display pictures and descriptions of highwaymen and, if you can find them, figures wearing the sorts of clothing that an innkeeper's daughter and an ostler would have worn.

PSHE and citizenship learning objective

◆ To recognise, as they approach puberty, how people's emotions change at that time and how to deal with their feelings towards themselves and others in a positive way (1d).

Background notes

This long poem tells the story of a landlord's daughter, Bess, and the highwayman whom she loves. She has an admirer, Tim the ostler, who overhears Bess and the highwayman declaring their love and tells the king's men about this. The king's men use Bess to lure the highwayman, but Bess manages to shoot herself first and, in doing so, warns the highwayman away to temporary safety. The extract tells of Tim overhearing the lovers' conversation and explores many issues that children face as they grow up. The discussions are aimed at Year 5 and 6 children and will highlight themes such as jealousy and what is right and wrong, tackling the ambiguity of moral issues, especially in matters of love.

Vocabulary

Characters, landlord, highwayman, ostler, jealously, betray, moral value.

Discussing the text

◆ Explain the background to the extract to place the characters in context. This is a difficult text, so begin by reading it to the children, drawing attention to the pace and emphasis of its rhythm. Then read it again, asking the children to join in when they feel confident.

◆ Ask for initial reactions to the text, for example the type of language used, its age, the descriptiveness.

◆ To explore the issues, the children need to understand the three characters – their types and the relationships between them. Go through the text, looking at each one in detail. Consider what a highwayman was. Demonstrate using a dictionary to check. What does he look like? What words suggest he is handsome and glamorous? Discuss specific features of his appearance, for example his *coat of the claret velvet*, and ensure all the children understand the descriptions. Then consider Bess. What might her job be? What might she be like? What evidence is there in the text? Although there are only a few clues in the extract, encourage the children to imagine what a landlord's daughter might wear at this time. If you can find one, show a picture to support this. Now look at Tim. What is an ostler? Again, use the dictionary to check. What judgements of him can the children make from the information given? What might he be like? (Point out phrases such as *His eyes were hollows of madness, his hair like mouldy hay.*) Do the children think his love for Bess would be returned? Why or why not?

◆ Having examined the characters, discuss the relationships and feelings between them.

PSHE and citizenship activities

◆ Discuss the relationship between the three characters in the poem. How do the children think Tim felt, realising that the woman he loved was in love with someone else? Could he compete for Bess's love? How would this add to how he felt? Make a list of words to describe the emotions he may have felt, for example *jealous, envious, unhappy, depressed.*

◆ Tell the children that sometimes in life, things don't work out the way we would like them to and, at some point, they will probably feel jealous of someone. Can they recall any such occasions? Ask the children to write about what happened and how they felt (or imagine a situation and how they would feel). What have they learned from it? For example, has there been a party that friends were invited to but they weren't? Was there a good reason, such as a limited number of people?

◆ Establish exactly what a highwayman was and discuss the moral values of this 'job'. Make links to Robin Hood, who became a hero. What was different about his situation? Did it make it any more right? What would be the modern day equivalent of a highwayman? Is it ever right to take things from other people? What about the saying *finders keepers*? The children need to be able to see both sides of a moral argument like this and understand that there are many and varied reasons why people do things that are (or seem) wrong. Ask the children to write about something wrong that they have done, explaining their motives.

◆ Make a class activity with a variety of scenarios described on cards. Make these have differing degrees of seriousness, for example pinching a rubber from a pencil case, driving after drinking and knocking someone down, being cheeky to an adult, beating someone up, stealing some fruit when really hungry. In groups, get the children to discuss the scenarios and decide whether the perpetrator of the crime is wrong or not. What should be the punishment? Ask the groups to report to the class. The children should find this difficult, as there are no 'black and white' answers, and it should help their awareness that right and wrong is not a straightforward judgement.

◆ Remind the children that Tim tells the king's men about the highwayman and Bess. Consider what his motive would be. Jealousy? Hatred? Or a sense of public duty? Was it the right thing to do? Talk about having to face difficult decisions as we get older and that there are often various possible solutions to one situation. Considering what to do for the best is difficult. Can the children use an example from their experience to illustrate this point? What solutions were available for the problem? Which did they choose and why? It is important for children to realise that when they were little, right and wrong were very straightforward concepts, but as we develop emotionally, these distinctions get blurred and difficult to judge. To emphasise how jealousy can make us behave oddly at times, ask the children to write a story about an occasion when they have felt jealous and acted out of character or did something questionable because of it.

◆ Use the drama technique of hot-seating, asking one child to be Tim the ostler. The rest of the class can then ask questions of him, focusing on finding out why he did what he did and the social and moral issues attached to his decision.

Further literacy ideas

◆ Using photocopies of the text, ask the children to highlight different ways in which the author creates atmosphere. Advise them to use a different colour highlighter for each method, for example alliteration and repetition. Also ask them to examine the rhythm and note down the number syllables in the lines of the text. Can the children find a pattern in each verse?

◆ In small groups, ask the children to brainstorm as many words as they can to describe people who commit crimes, for example *robber, thief, highwayman, murderer, criminal*. Then ask them to do the same for people who do good towards others or help others as part of their jobs, for example *vicar, nurse, nun, police officer, firefighter, charity volunteer*.

◆ Ask the children to rewrite the extract of text in play form and extend the story to include Tim informing the king's men about the highwayman and where to find him.

◆ The children could make a wanted poster for the highwayman. Look at the language used on posters and together pick out the important information from the text.

Genre
text messages

Disco 2night

Message from: Kate

HI HOW R U 2DAY? I AM SAD FEEL FED UP U?

Message from: Sam

Y U SAD? SUN IS SHINING GOT DISCO 2NGHT DEAD XCITED!

Message from: Kate

GOT SPOT ON NOSE AND JEY SAYS NOT GOING 2NGHT!! I DON'T THNK HE LIKES ME DO U?

Message from: Sam

IM SURE HE DOES BUT NOT MATTER ANYWAY U HAVE YOUR MATES!! WHAT WILL U WEAR? MUM SAYS I CAN STAY OUT UNTIL 9.30 U?

Message from: Kate

MY MUM WILL TAKE CAN YOURS PICK UP? THATS IF I GO!!!! WEARING JEANS + CROP TOP WITH SILVER SANDALS U?

Later

Message from: Sam

C J DOES LIKE U TALKED 2 U ALL NGHT! C U 2MORROW SX

Message from: Kate

TA GUD DO! KX

Disco 2night

Display the children's booklets on friendship and descriptions of their friends.

PSHE and citizenship learning objectives

◆ To recognise, as they approach puberty, how people's emotions change at that time and how to deal with their feelings towards themselves and others in a positive way (1d).

◆ To be aware of different types of relationship and develop skills to be effective in relationships (4c).

Vocabulary

Friendship, text messages, mates, shorthand.

Discussing the text

◆ Explore what the children already know about text messaging on mobile phones. Discuss who has sent messages. Who to? Do the children know anything about the special features of text messages, for example the shorthand, codes, icons and so on? (This is one area that the children will probably know more about than you!)

◆ Look at the texts together and establish who is having the 'conversation'. (There are options here of Sam being male or female, so ask the children to clarify why they think a certain way.) What might the relationship be between the two writers? What is the conversation about? Who is Sam?

◆ Discuss the content of the texts in detail and ask the children for their opinions on what may have happened in the interim between the two parts of the messages.

◆ How do the children think Kate feels after Sam's second message? (Reassured, comforted.) What does this tell us about the relationship between the two children? Help the children to appreciate that whatever happens between Kate and Jey, Sam will be her friend and there if needed.

PSHE and citizenship activities

◆ Kate and Sam are obviously close friends. What makes a close friend or best friend? Ask the children to write a list of instructions for being a best friend. These could be made into little books or leaflets to be displayed.

◆ Ask the children to write a description about their best friend or a good friend without mentioning the name. The writing can explain why they are a good friend, why they are good to be around, what special things they do and so on. These can then be illustrated and displayed, and others in the class can try to work out who each person is.

◆ Focus in on why Kate was fed up. Do the children ever have days when they feel like this? What things make them feel this way? (For example, broken friendships, Mum and Dad arguing, someone in the family being ill, an argument with someone, things not going right for them.) Ask pairs of children to make a list of what makes them sad or fed up. Then ask the pairs to share their ideas with the class to make a class list. Are the ideas generally the same?

◆ Look at the class list of things that make us fed up. For each reason on the list, try to find suggestions for how we could help someone who was feeling sad for that particular reason. What could we say or do to help them feel better or cared for? For example if the reason is *had an argument*, the advice might be to encourage them to talk to the person they have argued with and apologise, explaining without getting cross again how they feel.

◆ As we grow up, our friends and the things we like to do with our friends change. Ask the children to write about a friend that they had when they were little and what they liked doing with that friend. Tell them to compare this with what they like doing now (with the same friend or a newer one).

◆ What do the children like to do in their leisure time? How often are they able to do it? Is it something they do on their own, with friends or with someone from their family? Brainstorm a list of activities as a class, then ask individuals to choose their favourite one or two to write a description of. Encourage them to emphasise in their writing *why* they like doing that activity.

Further literacy ideas

◆ Look at the way the text is written. Discuss the use of appropriate language for a particular purpose. Introduce or remind the children of the terms *standard English* and *dialect* and talk about a variety of circumstances that would be appropriate for each. What sort of language is used in text messaging? (A kind of shorthand.) Why has this language developed? (There are a limited number of characters that can make up a message; the number of buttons are a physically awkward way of making up words; it is time-consuming.) Emphasise that full sentences are not needed, that words, and often letters, are left out, but the meaning is still clear. There are actually text messaging code books published. Ask if any of the children has one that you could look at together.

◆ Ask the children in groups to make lists of conventional spellings and the corresponding text shorthand versions.

◆ Discuss the shorthand style where vowels are missing and why some words are still relatively easy to read when they are in context, even without the vowels. Investigate which words would work in this way.

◆ Look at other times when we write quick, short, messages or notes, for example telephone messages, reminder notes, secret messages to friends. How are they written?

◆ Investigate codes with the children and ask pairs to make up their own code.

Relationships and respecting differences

This chapter combines two themes – relationships, particularly within families and between friends, and respecting difference, a key requirement of equal opportunities education.

Relationships are formed and developed usually between people with a common interest or goal, or because of mutual self-interest. Even amongst families, where most relationships are predetermined only by blood ties, skills are needed to preserve constructive warmth and harmony. Three factors are necessary for the maintenance of relationships: open and honest communication, empathy, and commitment. The texts in this chapter examine some of the problems inherent in family relationships, the problem of brothers and the complex dynamics of adopted children. The need for loyalty is examined in 'A friend in need'. 'I am David' is an examination of the problem of cruelty and misuse and their impact on forming relationships.

The PSHE and citizenship syllabus requires that children understand the rights and responsibilities inherent in relationships and to consider that sometimes these conflict with one another. It also asks teachers to help children acquire the skills needed to be good friends.

Respecting differences is a key component of equal opportunities education. Differences of gender, race, culture and disability need to be considered and discussed with the children. In society today, stereotypes are still apparent and some people still make judgements of other people based on these stereotypes. The work in this area of PSHE and citizenship will help children have a broader, more balanced view of individuals and their role in society, irrespective of gender, culture, religion, race or disability. It will help them to value each and every person for their positive qualities and understand that we are all different from one another whilst having the same basic feelings and needs. The variety of cultures, traditions and values are to be celebrated and encompassed into a rich, diverse society. These texts don't specifically tackle gender issues, but there are many good texts available that do explore this topic. The principles remain the same: making suppositions or value judgements about a person based on their sex is wrong.

Brothers

Genre
poems based
on common
themes

Objection

My feelings towards my little brother
Would soften
If only, once every so often,
He'd blow his nose.

He's not without style.
Why won't he, just once in a while,
Do you suppose?

As things are,
I just can't stick it.
Why can't he blow it
Instead of pick it?

Kit Wright

Tricks

Nearly every morning
my brother would lie in bed,
lift his hands up in the air
full stretch
then close his hands around an invisible bar.
"Ah, my magic bar," he'd say.
Then he'd heave on the bar,
pull himself up,
until he was sitting up in bed.

Then he'd get up.
I said,
"You haven't got a magic bar above your bed."
"I have," he said.
"You haven't," I said.
"Don't believe me then," he said.
"I won't – don't worry," I said.
"It doesn't make any difference to me
if you do or you don't," he said,
and went out of the room.

"Magic bar!" I said.
"Mad. He hasn't got a magic bar."
I made sure he'd gone downstairs,
then I walked over to his bed
and waved my hand about in the air
above his pillow.
"I knew it," I said to myself.
"Didn't fool me for a moment."

Michael Rosen

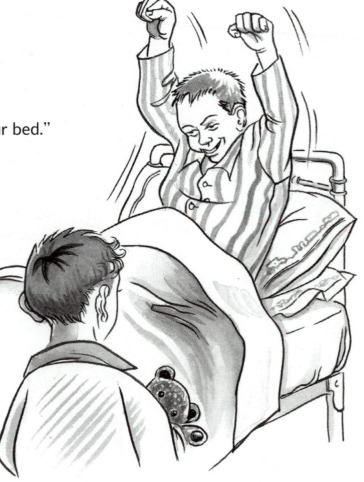

Brothers

Make a *Brothers are…* display with adjectives alongside a matching *Sisters are…* display.

PSHE and citizenship learning objectives

◆ To set personal goals in relation to changing their habits and behaviour (1b).

◆ To realise the consequences of anti-social behaviours, particularly playing tricks on people (2c).

◆ To resolve differences (2f).

◆ To be aware of different types of relationship, including marriage and those between friends and families, and to develop the skills to be effective in relationships (4c).

◆ To understand that using imagination in play is fine, but that we also need real friends and family to be with.

Vocabulary

Habits, tricks, make a fool of, annoying, hurtful, irritating.

Discussing the text

◆ Read the poem 'Objection' with the children. Ask them what they thought about it. Did they like it? Was it clever? What sort of poem is it? (Humorous.)

◆ What is it that the 'speaker' of the poem doesn't like about his or her brother? Do the children have any brothers or sisters or cousins with annoying habits? (You might have to subdue or gloss over the more graphic examples!) Why are some habits annoying? (Perhaps because they are so familiar, or are unsavoury.)

◆ What is a habit? (A repeated action, something you always do, for example get out of bed the same side, clean you teeth a certain way, tap your spoon on the table.)

◆ Ask the children: *If you have a habit that upsets or irritates your family or friends, should you try to change it?* (Allow a range of answers as long as they are reasoned. Suggest that on the one hand, learning to live with others and their habits is part of any successful relationship – after all, they have annoying habits too; on the other hand, if someone is doing something habitually that offends, breaking the habit will help the relationship.) From this discussion, draw out the need for effort and compromise in relationships.

◆ Read the poem 'Tricks' with the children, introducing it as another poem about a brother. Ask the children which poem they like best and why. (Some may favour Michael Rosen's because of its well-crafted structure and straightforward narrative. Others may prefer Kit Wright's unorthodox yet rhythmic structure and its subject matter.)

◆ Establish what is happening in this poem. (A brother tricks his sibling by pretending to have a magic bar above his bed.)

◆ Is the brother really tricking his sibling or is he just pretending for his own pleasure? Is he wrong to make the claim about the magic bar? (If it is deliberately to make fun, then it probably is. If it is just his own fantasy, then probably not.) Draw out the moral benchmark that things are wrong if hurt is done to someone else or themselves by their actions, what they say and what they don't say.

◆ What would make the brother's actions much more harmful? (For example, he might laugh at his sibling or tell his friends about how silly he was, making a fool of him.)

◆ Do any of the children have brothers or sisters or cousins who like to trick them? How does it make them feel? Do they play tricks back?

◆ Discuss how you can deal with a sibling who frequently tries tricks like this. Help the children to understand that, first, a direct but firm request to stop needs to be made. Then, and probably because the first fails, the best approach is not to react to the 'joke', but ignore and dismiss it. Help the children see that the trickster gets pleasure from the trouble he or she can cause, so reducing the fuss usually reduces the likelihood of further pranks. However, remind them that, if necessary, they shouldn't be afraid to call on adult help.

P *SHE and citizenship activities*

◆ Individually, ask the children to think about all the habits they have. Do they have any that irritate or annoy their family? Ask them to write a plan of action for changing that habit. How are they going to stop themselves? Who can help them and how? They could then share their action plans with their families and follow them.

◆ In pairs, give the children this scene to role-play: *One of your friends has a bad habit and you tell them that you find it annoying and you want to help them stop it. How does your friend react? What happens then?*

◆ Ask the children to write a poem about how it feels to be tricked and laughed at. In the final verse, they should write about what they intend to do about being tricked.

◆ Tell the children to look up the meaning of *practical joker*. They should write an explanation for this phrase and, under two headings, list what's good about living with a practical joker and what's bad.

◆ As a whole class, talk about make-believe and pretend. Say that we often use our imaginations to enjoy ourselves, and that's alright as long as it doesn't keep us apart from other people. Illustrate this with an example like the magic bar in 'Tricks', but emphasise the example of imaginary friends that younger children sometimes have. Ask the children to write a story, from the point of view of an older sibling, about a boy or girl who has a pretend friend. Ask: *How do you help your brother or sister? Do you tell him that his friend isn't real, do you go along with it, or do you help him to find real friends?*

◆ In mixed-sex groups, tell the children to discuss what it is like to have brothers or sisters. (Children that don't have siblings can imagine what it would be like.) To make or add to the display, ask each group to make a spider diagram of the characteristics around *Brothers are…* or *Sisters are…* Then ask everyone to feed their results back to the class. Conclude by confirming that having siblings has advantages and disadvantages and that they would say the same about us.

Further literacy ideas

◆ In small groups, tell the children to share as many nasty or disgusting habits as can be thought of. Then, in pairs, encourage them to write a poem about some of these habits, under the title 'Please don't do that!'. You could go on to compare the children's poems with 'Tricks' and some of Roald Dahl's 'disgusting' characters, for example the Twits.

◆ Help the children to construct a wordsearch or crossword, using key nouns or verbs drawn from the two poems and test it out on their friends.

◆ Look at the phrasing of both poems. How do they contrast and in what ways are they similar? Look particularly at the number of lines per verse and the use of rhyme endings.

Andy's Big Question

Andy was adopted when he was three years old.

Genre
*contemporary
fiction, a story
in a familiar
setting that
raises issues*

Now Andy is ten. Because his family is a foster family, lots of children come and go. But not everyone leaves. Sara and Laura were born to this family. They are at secondary school now and will live at home until they are grown up.

Andy doesn't look like Sara and Laura. He doesn't look like Mum and Dad either. But he is just as much part of their family. Being adopted means, 'I belong.'

Sometimes Andy is not sure he likes belonging to this busy family. If he thinks really hard he can almost remember his first mum. When he gets angry with Mum and Dad he sometimes thinks he'd rather be with her.

One Tuesday night, Andy was sitting at the long kitchen table with his homework. Dad was marking essays and Mum was washing up. Andy looked out of the window. The dogs lay snoozing in the evening sun. It would soon be dark.

Andy couldn't see why anybody needed to know about a stupid war that happened hundreds of years ago. So he played with his pencil, and looked at the pictures in his book. Finally he closed his book with a loud slap and said, "I've finished." Then he scooted out of the back door to play.

Ten minutes later Dad stormed out with Andy's exercise book in his hand.

"Andy, come here," he bellowed. "If you did your homework, you wrote in invisible ink. How about doing it again properly? And since you think going out to play is so important, there'll be no more outside play this week!"

Andy felt a red rush of anger building up his back all the way to the top of his head.

"The whole week?" he yelled. "Just because of one rotten piece of homework?"

He grabbed his homework book and shouted, "I hate homework. My real mum wouldn't make me do it. I know she wouldn't. I want to go and live with her!" Then he ran into the house, slammed the door, and ran up to his room.

Andy kicked his waste-paper basket. Then he kicked his chest-of-drawers and punched his pillow. After a while he felt the anger prickles fading from his neck. He leaned back against his pillow and stared out of the window.

"Why did I get so angry?" Andy wondered. Two things came to mind: school and his mother – not the mum downstairs peeling apples for tomorrow's pies, but his first mum. Just lately it seemed as if every time he thought about school or his first mum, he got in a temper. He got in a temper about school because he never seemed to do as well as Sara and Laura, or even as well as Mum and Dad expected him to. And he got in a temper about Mum – for thousands of reasons, most of which he couldn't spell out.

Later that night, Andy's dad came upstairs and sat next to Andy on his bed. Andy showed Dad the homework he'd now done – all ready for tomorrow. Dad checked each answer as carefully as he checked his own pupils' history essays. Then he put his arm around Andy.

"Do you sometimes miss your first mum?" he asked quietly.

Andy felt a lump in his throat so big that he couldn't talk. He just nodded his head. He wished he could tell his dad the hundred questions that crowded his mind.

Dad sat still and held him for a while. But when Andy didn't say anything, he left and closed the door. Andy heard his dad's footsteps get softer down each stair. He looked at the smiling faces of his family in the photo propped up on the chest-of-drawers. There he stood between Sara and Laura, with Dad's arm on his shoulder and Mum on the other side. But did he really belong in that smiling group?

Carolyn Nystrom

Andy's Big Question

Make a display of different types of families, illustrated and captioned. You could also display a class guide to fostering and adoption.

PSHE and citizenship learning objectives

◆ To recognise their worth as individuals by identifying positive things about themselves (1b).

◆ To recognise, as they approach puberty, that their emotions change and how to deal with their feelings towards themselves, their family and others in a positive way (1d).

◆ To be aware of different types of relationship, including marriage and those between friends and families, and to develop the skills to be effective in relationships (4c).

◆ To know where individuals and families can get help and support (4g).

◆ To know that adoption and fostering can be a very positive experience and that children can be loved and nurtured by people other than their blood-relatives.

Background notes

This story deals with some of the conflicting emotions that can arise where children are adopted or fostered. If there are children in the class who have been adopted or who are currently with foster parents, care will be needed in deciding how you use the text.

Vocabulary

Adoption, fostering, abandonment, anger, fear, blood-relative.

Discussing the text

◆ Read the sentence of introduction. Ask the children what they understand by adoption. How does a child come to be adopted? Explore a range of reasons, but present them in as positive a way as possible, for example parents may have died in an accident and there is no one else in the family who can look after the child or parent(s) may feel unable to care for the child properly and that he or she would have a better life with a new family.

◆ Read the first paragraph. What is fostering? How different is this to adoption. Again, stress the positive aspects, not the temporary nature of fostering as a by-product of not being wanted.

◆ Read the next paragraph. Draw a family tree for Andy, with his real mum connected to him but to one side of his adoptive family, to help the children understand the relationships. At the bottom of the diagram, record the sentence *Being adopted means 'I belong.'*

◆ Read the rest of the extract. Why does Andy get angry when he thinks of school? Prompt the children to use the text to help them. Why does Andy worry about not being as good as Laura and Sara? Does he feel he has to do as well as them to please his new parents? Why does he worry that he's not living up to their expectations? (Perhaps he thinks they'll get rid of him or he feels he has to be very good to thank them for taking him in.)

◆ Discuss the children's ideas about why Andy gets angry when he thinks about his mum. (This is sensitive, but the ideas will be valuable.)

◆ How can Andy's new parents help him with these feelings? (By reassuring him that he needs only to do his best, they will love him and keep a safe place for him always. Also, perhaps, by encouraging him to talk through his feelings about his mum. It may even be appropriate to arrange a meeting with his mother, or write a letter to her.) Make the final point that sometimes we can love someone very much but still be angry with them. We may need to talk to them to find out why they did things. At the very least, we need to talk to others about our angry feelings and frustrations. We need friends and family to listen and show that they care for us.

◆ Ask the children what they think will happen next in the story.

PSHE and citizenship activities

◆ Ask the children to write a conclusion to the story. What happens to Andy? How does he resolve his feelings? (In the rest of the story, Andy talks with his adoptive parents about his need to know why he was adopted and who his parents were. His new parents are able to help him understand that his mother was young and alone and couldn't earn enough money to look after him. She loved him very much. They also give Andy a photograph of his mum holding him when he was little.)

◆ Talk about why Andy's real mum may have given him away for adoption – including her age and lack of money. Ask the children to write two diary entries from her point of view – one just before she has to take her son to the new family and one just after.

◆ Andy has two mums and one dad, and two sisters and other 'temporary' brothers and sisters. What are the advantages of this arrangement? In pairs, ask the children to come up with a list of the good things about being in a foster or adoptive family.

◆ In groups, ask the children to discuss and list the qualities needed to be good foster or adoptive parents. Ask each group to feed back to the class, justifying the characteristics they noted.

◆ Invite a member of Social Services to come in and explain how they find foster and adoptive homes for children. Alternatively, or as well, you could ask a foster parent to talk about what it is like to have foster children and why they do it.

◆ In groups of three, help the children to role-play a situation where a friend seems very down and angry. When someone asks what is wrong, he or she eventually explains it is because he is adopted. How does he feel? How do the other children help him?

◆ Together, look at the diversity of family types. Ask the children to come up with as many variations as they can, including, for example, a one-parent family and an extended family. Then allocate each type to a small group of children to provide a description and illustration for the display.

Further literacy ideas

◆ Using information books from the library, ask the children to write a simple guide to fostering and adoption. Let them word-process the text and print it off, putting it into a class guide to adoption and fostering.

◆ Look at other forms of adoption, such as adopting an animal at the zoo, or a child in the Third World. What does this involve? How else is the term *adoption* used? (To take up an idea or practice.) Ask the children to write a number of sentences using the term *adoption* in different contexts.

◆ Tell the children to rewrite the extract as a series of Andy's journal entries.

A friend in need

Genre
contemporary
fiction that
raises issues,
serial story

It was the first day of a new school year. Everyone was in the Hall for assembly.

"Before you return to your classes," the headteacher intoned, "I want you to know that one of our children, by his prompt and courageous actions, has earned a 'Good Citizenship' award from the Civic Society. Jeremy Ford, come up please."

There was loud applause, led by Paul and Ajay, Jez's mates. Only the teachers preserved their stony expressions. An award to the infamous Year 6 boy Jeremy Ford? Impossible!

Jez stood alongside the headteacher, an embarrassed grin upon his face.

"This boy, standing before you," the headteacher boomed, his heavy hand landing with weight upon Jez's shoulder, "wrestled two armed thieves to the floor, made a citizens arrest and kept the men pinned down until the police arrived. Jeremy, we at Hollingsfield Junior School are proud of you."

There was a cacophony of cheers, whistles, drumming and vigorous clapping as Jez raised his fist in salute. Only two classmates refused to join in.

"It's time we did something about Jez," Simon whispered. "He's getting above himself." His sidekick Gary, nodded enthusiastically. All that remained was to find a way of dealing with Jez without getting hurt or caught!

Three days later at morning break, Simon watched as Jez finally left the classroom. Once the boy had sprinted out of sight, everything was set for the execution of Simon's plan. He took out his new computer game. Children were not allowed to bring such valuables into school in case they were damaged or lost, but Simon had something else in mind. His game was going to be stolen, stolen by Jez.

"Miss, I can't find my computer game. I left it in my bag. It isn't there now."

That was how it started, so simple, so clever. A search of the cloakroom was conducted. Simon acted his part astonishingly well, sorrow, worry, disbelief, even the teacher was taken in.

"Never mind. We'll have a proper look at lunch," she finally declared. It wasn't until the groups were given their literacy tasks and sent to their places that Simon's plot came to fulfilment.

"Ajay, get my book," Jez had called.

"Sure thing!"

The whole class, a hubbub of noise and movement miraculously froze

into stillness and silence as Dave held in his hand a computer game.

"That's mine!" Simon yelled.

"Ajay?" the teacher queried, moving relentlessly towards the desk.

Ajay shot a sick, helpless look towards his friend. Jez seemed unaware of the danger. He was watching with as much fascination as anyone was.

"Where did you find this?" the teacher demanded quietly.

Ajay winced then said, "In the tray."

"Jeremy's tray?"

An incredulous laugh made every one jump. Jez thought it was funny. The teacher's look of anger and shock changed that.

"Do me a favour!" Jez began indignantly, "What would I want with that…"

"Everyone, take out your reading books and read in silence. Simon, Jeremy, come with me."

Jez jerked to his feet, scattering classmates around as he did. He was ready to strike out. His temper all but blown. From the safety of the teacher's far side, Simon smiled. It wasn't until then that Jez understood what kind of trouble he was in.

Simon came back into class at lunchtime. Jez did not. His two friends were already certain that Jez hadn't taken anything. That

was confirmed when Simon passed by with a smug triumphant grin on his face.

"What have you done?" Ajay shouted, his fist clutching at Simon's sweatshirt.

"Ajay, leave it!" Paul appealed. "The dinner helper's coming."

That night Ajay and Paul called at Jez's house.

"Come to gloat!" Jez began.

The good-natured Paul suddenly lost his temper. "Shut up Jez! We've come to help!"

Jez wiped his face with his hand, then raked his fingers through his hair.

"I'm suspended, until some meeting or other when they'll chuck me out. Good Citizen. Joke, eh?"

"Simon set you up. Didn't they see that?"

The reply was a stark, "No."

"We'll think of something Jez," Paul eventually said. It didn't sound very hopeful.

The following day Paul tried direct appeal to Miss Kelly. To her credit she listened, acknowledged that Simon could have planted the game but that it wasn't likely. "Jeremy is impulsive," she said. Paul had no answer to that. Miss Kelly concluded the interview with a warning.

"Don't talk to Simon, or threaten him. I don't want to see you get into trouble."

So the authorities wouldn't

listen and forcing a confession from Simon was out of the question. Time to think again.

Think the boys did, but to no avail. The day of the meeting came. By two o'clock the governors of the school would be assembled with Jez and his mother to decide Jez's fate.

Ajay and Paul forewent the football at lunch. Their hearts weren't in it. They had failed Jez; failed themselves as well. Seated outside the open door of the Year Four class, the two boys were annoyed to see Gary, Simon's sidekick, idling over, a smirk on his face.

"Said goodbye to Jez then?" Gary taunted.

"Shut it Gary," growled Ajay, his fists tight.

Gary scowled but behind the irritation was fear. Simon had gone too far. It wasn't funny any more. He dropped down to sit beside them.

"Si's very clever," Gary began.

"Si's a sneaking, ratting little…"

Paul thumped Ajay in the stomach to shut him up. He'd seen out of the corner of his eye Mr Cox, Class Four's teacher, hovering inside the doorway. Unbeknown to Gary, the teacher was eavesdropping.

A small smile flickered on Paul's face as Gary went on speaking his troubled mind.

"Si's all right. He's just gone too far with this consul joke, that's all. I told Si he should own up, or say it was all a mistake."

Ajay snorted. Gary never contradicted Simon, never did anything other than agree with his friend and trail after him.

Gary mumbled on. "He wants Jez out of the school. 'Getting too big for his boots,' he said. It's not my fault Jez is getting chucked out."

Mr Cox had heard enough. Gary started in fright as the teacher's hand gripped his arm from behind.

"We'd better have a talk, Gary. Don't you agree?"

Paul and Ajay met up with Jez after school. Laser battles and McDonald's for all of them, Mrs Ford had announced.

"I don't know how you did it, but I owe you," Jez declared. The three boys shared a happy grin then bolted.

Gillian Goddard

A friend in need

Make a display on friendship, with a picture of Jez and his two friends, Paul and Ajay, surrounded by key phrases that tell us what is needed in a good friend.

PSHE and citizenship learning objectives

◆ To know why rules and laws are made and enforced (2b).

◆ To understand that there are different kinds of responsibilities, rights and duties at school and between friends, and that these sometimes conflict with one another (2d).

◆ To know that pressure to behave in an unacceptable or risky way can come from a variety of sources, including people they know, and how to ask for help and resist pressure to do wrong (3f).

◆ To develop the skills to be effective in friendships (4c).

Background notes

This story has the same lead character as 'Look before you leap' in 'Keeping safe and healthy' and 'Set a thief to catch a thief' in the chapter on citizenship. Indeed, 'Set a thief to catch a thief' is the story of how Jez comes to win the 'Good Citizenship' award. Use the stories together to challenge stereotypes, suggest how a troublemaker can be reformed and examine the nature of friendship.

Vocabulary

Theft, stealing, plant, crime, reputation, loyalty, injustice.

Discussing the text

◆ Read the first part of the story with the children, to the point where Simon and Gary have resolved to do something about Jez *without getting hurt or caught!* Ask the children why the teachers are less than keen on applauding Jeremy (Jez) Ford. Find the words that tell us: *An award to the infamous Year 6 boy Jeremy Ford? Impossible!* What sort of things might Jez usually get up to? Why had Jez received this award? (For tackling two thieves and stopping a crime.)

◆ Is Jez popular amongst his schoolmates? (Yes.) How do we know? (The positive reaction in the assembly.) Why do they think he is popular with the children, but not with the teachers? Discuss differing points of view and what adults, particularly teachers, like in children and the qualities children like in each other. Record these on a flip chart.

◆ Why do Simon and Gary want to *do something about* Jez? (Probably jealousy). What do the children think they are going to try and do?

◆ Read the next part of the story, up to the confrontation at lunchtime. Clarify what has happened. (Simon has planted a computer game on Jez, then reported it stolen. Ajay accidentally finds the game in Jez's desk and it seems to the teacher that Jez must have stolen the game.) What is likely to happen to Jez? (He is in serious trouble. He may be suspended then possibly expelled for stealing. There is also the possibility of criminal charges.) Ask the children what is so serious about theft and reinforce the need to respect one another's property.

◆ Ask the children if they think Jez will be believed. Why not? (There's 'proof' in the desk and Jez has a reputation for getting into trouble.) Discuss the problem of carrying a bad reputation. Did Simon know this when he acted? (Yes, he knew they would believe him rather than Jez.) Introduce the idea of injustice and explain what it means.

◆ Read the story to the end. How did Paul and Ajay manage to help Jez? (First by supporting and believing him and keeping him company – being loyal, then by finding a legitimate way of tricking Gary into a confession when a teacher could overhear.)

◆ Ask the children which is the worse wrongdoing – taking the game or deliberately planting it on someone to get him into trouble for theft. (Allow a range of responses here, as long as the children recognise the reasons for actions and the intent to harm. They should conclude that both are wrong.)

PSHE and citizenship activities

◆ Discuss the qualities of friendship shown by Paul and Ajay and record them on the flip chart. Prepare these for display with each small group taking a quality of a good friend and providing an illustration and explanation or example.

◆ With older children, discuss the times when loyalty to friends might be misplaced, such as Gary's initial loyalty to Simon. Tell the children to role-play a situation when friends stay loyal to someone who has done wrong. Then ask them to perform the scene with the friends doing the right thing. What should people do if one of their friends is doing wrong? (Tell them to stop it and make amends, or tell them they must own up. Stress that they can no longer be friends if they persist in wrongdoing.) This is very difficult. Like Gary, it's tempting to do nothing, but it made him very miserable.

◆ In pairs, ask the children to write an explanation of why theft is wrong. Make the point that protection of property is a common social rule that crosses all cultures and faiths.

◆ Ask half the class to rewrite the story from Simon's point of view, and the other half from Gary's. Ensure the children appreciate that the two boys are different and this should be reflected in their tales. Simon is the leader and initiator of the idea. Gary goes along with the idea but then thinks better of it. He is too frightened to tell a teacher, but does talk with Jez's mates. This leads to justice.

◆ In groups, ask the children to discuss Simon's motivation. Did his feelings towards Jez excuse his actions? (No.) Tell them to role-play a dialogue between the headteacher and Simon as he is 'brought to book' for his trickery, exposing these reasons.

◆ Ask the children to write a story about someone with a bad reputation who was blamed for something he or she didn't do. How did she feel? Encourage them to end the story on a positive note.

Further literacy ideas

◆ Consider vocabulary that has come up in the discussions and together list as many opposites as possible using the addition of prefixes. For example justice – injustice, sane – insane, helpful – unhelpful, comfortable – uncomfortable, loyal – disloyal, harmony – disharmony, compliance – noncompliance.

◆ Let the children word-process the dialogue between Simon and the headteacher in play form.

◆ Look at the use of name contractions such as those used in the story. Using examples from the children, construct a chart of long and short names.

◆ In pairs, see if the children can write a simple moral guide for Year 2 children to help them avoid getting into trouble. Tell them to focus on telling the truth, getting a good reputation and respecting other people's property.

◆ Compare this story with 'Set a thief to catch a thief' on page 154. What do these two stories have in common? What sort of stories are these (Serial stories – they follow one another with the same lead characters.) Ask the children to find the difference between serial stories and story series. Look at other serials, including those on television, where the same characters have different adventures each week. In pairs, ask the children to contrive a two-episode serial around two key characters. Explain that you want each member of the pair to write one episode. Remind them that the characters have to remain common and the second episode must follow on chronologically from the first.

I am David

Genre
*historical
fiction*

"I'll help you to find your spectacles."

David stepped slowly forward. "Here they are," he said, and added hesitantly, "Sir." The man put the glasses on and smiled again, and David felt sure he was not one of *them*. He had quite a different look about him: David could not imagine him striking or shooting anyone. He now felt in his pocket, took something out and offered it to David. A coin lay in his hand. "You must have something for your trouble," he said.

"No," said David quickly, stepping back. "I mean – no, thank you."

The stranger looked a little disconcerted, then he smiled and said in that case David must accept his thanks and asked if he would like to say, "How do you do?" to his wife.

———————

Then the woman suggested they should have something she called 'sandwiches'. These turned out to be food – slices of bread with something between them. They asked David if he would like one, and he said "Yes, please."

They seemed pleased when David accepted their offer, and David thought they might be willing to answer a question if he put one to them.

"Is there a king in England?" he inquired.

The man told him at the moment there was a queen because the last king had no sons, only daughters. She was a good queen, he said, and beautiful, too, and she had a very fine golden crown.

David looked at him in surprise. What did it matter what she had? All that really mattered was that the people of England were free, as people always were in those countries that had kings – or, of course, queens.

He ate the last mouthful. "I've finished, sir. Can I go now?"

The woman leaned over towards him. "Yes, of course you can. But... David, I would like to see you smile."

David felt awkward: her face had an anxious look, as if she were waiting for him to give her something. But he had nothing to give.

"I... I'm sorry: I don't know how to do it."

He turned away slightly and asked again, "Can I go now, sir?"

———————

"Won't you let me go? I didn't take your food before you said I could."

"Of course you may go, David." the man's voice sounded almost like Johannes. "If there were any way in which we could help you, you would tell us, wouldn't you?"

"Yes, sir. There isn't. Thank you. Good-bye." He was in such a hurry to get away, he stumbled over his words. Then off he ran before they could stop him. He ran back along the road, and before he reached the first bend he lay down in the ditch and looked back at the car. It stayed there a long time before it drove off.

It was growing quite dark now.

David began to clamber slowly down the slope towards the sea to find himself a place to sleep in for the night. He was thinking about the strangers – English people from a free country. They were obviously kind, and yet they did not seem willing to let him go, especially the woman. She seemed to think she ought to keep him there. David could not understand it... but when he searched his mind for what he knew about countries that were free, he found the answer: in those countries they had a kind of police force to help those who had not done anything wrong. She was only there on holiday, and perhaps she had no idea how different things were in other countries. The thought was comforting: he had been alarmed at the idea that she would deliberately set out to ensnare him – there would be a sort of treachery in giving him food and smiling at him and then seeking to hold on to him. But if she were ignorant of the situation, then there was nothing sinister in what she had done. Only he must take more care and remember not to look at people long enough for them to notice his eyes. It would be helpful to find a mirror – if he knew what was wrong with his eyes he might be able to do something about it. And he would have to learn to smile: people had sometimes smiled at him in the town, and then they had looked put out as if they regretted having done it. If you could smile back every time people smiled at you, perhaps they would take less notice of you.

Anne Holm

I am David

Put up a map of Europe with David's route outlined. In front of it, display copies of *I am David*, Anne Frank's *Diary of a Young Girl* and Ian Serraillier's *The Silver Sword* if you have them. You might also want to include pictures of concentration camps that are not too shocking and a wall display of a camp fence and buildings, surrounded by feelings words, such as *fear*, *pain*, *hate*, *defeat*, *loss despair* and labelled *Imprisonment*. Add to this a scene of a road, trees, hills and sunlight with a signpost to Denmark, labelled *Freedom* and add words like *confusion*, *joy*, *puzzlement*, *love*, *care* and others suggested by the children.

PSHE and citizenship learning objectives
◆ To discuss and debate topical issues and events (2a).
◆ To realise the consequences of anti-social and aggressive behaviours on individuals (2c).
◆ To think about the lives of people living in other places and times (4b).
◆ To be aware of different types of relationship and develop skills to be effective in relationships (4c).

Background notes
These extracts are useful to link to the history and geography curricula. They are from a very powerful book describing a boy's survival and rediscovery of life after imprisonment in a concentration camp. Although the book does not dwell on camp experiences, it does focus on very traumatic situations and emotions and would work best with a Year 6 class that is fairly mature. The extracts here highlight the problem of building up trust with strangers and ultimately of breaching self-imposed isolation.

Explain to the children that a boy called David has been imprisoned for most of his young life in a concentration camp during World War II. He doesn't know anything about himself, who he is, where he comes from or who his family is. All he knows is that his name is David. He suffered a great deal in the camp and saw many terrible things, but he had one friend and guide, a man called Johannes. Unfortunately the man died, leaving David defenceless and alone. When the commander of the camp offers to help him escape, he takes the chance, sure that this was a cruel trick. It wasn't. He did get away and ran for days and nights south to Salonica, then north through Italy to get to Denmark, where the commander had told him to go. Terrified of being captured, David tries to avoid all contact with people, yet he needs help to survive. He is hiding by a rough road in Italy when a car pulls up. The driver gets out and David hears him mutter, in English, about losing his glasses.

Vocabulary
Imprisonment, concentration camp, freedom, trust, mistrust, fear, loneliness, kindness, holocaust.

Discussing the text
◆ Introduce the context of the story, with the mass imprisonment of Jews and other peoples (men, women and children) in camps. Explain what the term means in this context and mention the appalling treatment that most of the inmates met, including deliberate starvation and killing. Ask the children what they know about these camps, if anything.
◆ Explain the background to the story and what is happening when the first extract begins. Ask the children why the commander might have wanted David to get away. Try to get them to consider darker motives rather than a liking for the boy. (In fact the camp was due to be liberated very soon.)

◆ Read the first few lines, up to *David could not imagine him striking or shooting anyone*. Ask the children what David meant when he thought that this man was not one of *them*. Why did he offer to help the man? What does this tell us about David's character? What reassured David that this man was safe? Discuss what we know so far about David's experience of *them*.

◆ Read to the end of page. Discuss the problems David has in coping with kind people. Why can't David smile? Even if he does learn to smile, what purpose will it serve in his own mind? (To ensure he doesn't draw attention to himself. It is a defensive/protective mechanism.) Would this work, do they think? David refused to accept the gift of money, yet he needed money to get food. Why did he do this? Was he right? (He believed it was right to do things without expecting reward. Money would spoil his gift of help.) Allow the children to express their views about the correctness of refusing money. Ultimately, because this mattered to David – it was a principle by which he governed his life, he was right to refuse.

◆ Finally, ask children what might happen to David. Allow them a full range of responses.

PSHE and citizenship activities

◆ Ask the children to write a poem in two verses, the first using feelings words associated with the camp experience for David, the second with his feelings once he was free.

◆ Ask the children to write a sequel to the story extract describing the next episode in David's adventure. How does he cope when he next meets people? Does he use his smile? Does he make friends or remain afraid of people?

◆ In pairs, get the children to role-play a conversation between the husband and wife in the car after they leave David. What are their thoughts and feelings about this disturbing young boy? What will they do? (For example, forget about it, go back to try to help him or report him to officials.)

◆ In small groups, ask the children to discuss why the German authorities imprisoned people and treated them this way. Why was it wrong? (It is wrong to deny people freedom, hurt them, deliberately neglect them, be cruel to them and kill them, especially when they had done nothing wrong, but were simply of a different cultural or religious group, or had different views to those in power.)

◆ As a whole class, discuss whether the detainment of asylum seekers in prisons and detention centres today is also wrong. What are the differences? (They are not deliberately hurt, starved, beaten or killed, but their freedom is denied.) Alternatively, the issue of the imprisonment of criminals could be considered, if preferred. Neither of these situations is parallel to German concentration camps and the differences must be delineated. Nevertheless, the issues of infringement of basic human rights can still be addressed.

◆ Invite a well-selected speaker in to talk about the impact of the holocaust on victims or visit an art exhibition on the holocaust. You could try education officers and the Manchester Jewish Museum on 0161 834 9879.

Further literacy ideas

◆ Help the children, in threes, to translate the extracts into a play format, with stage directions. The groups could then act their written scenes to the rest of class.

◆ Ask the children to compare this story with those of Anne Frank's diary or *The Silver Sword*, using reviews or the books' blurb. What parallels are there in content and experiences and what differences? Ask the children to provide their own blurb for *I am David* based on the extract and discussions.

◆ Towards the end of the second extract, look at the use of the pause or hesitation in the text. What punctuation device is used for this? (An ellipsis, made up of three dots.) Write up this example from the text, then ask the children to write two more similar sentences of their own.

The Trouble With Josh

Genre
contemporary
fiction
including
information
text

"Joshua McDermitt, you come down. Now! Do you hear me?" I knew it wouldn't do an ounce of good, but I had to try.

I saw Josh standing right on the ridge of our house with his arms flapping fast like wings.

"Whooo, whooo, whooo," he yelled, his voice shrill enough to be heard down the street at Butch Carlin's house. "I can fly, Katie! I can fly! I'm a bird. I'm a plane. I'm Superman!"

Josh teetered on the roof, and took a few unsteady skids down the slope. I covered my eyes and waited for the thud, but it didn't come. He must have grabbed hold of something because, when I dared to look, Josh was back on the ridge again, being a bird, a plane, and Superman – all at once.

I didn't know how he'd climbed up there but, after nearly nine years of living with Josh, I'd believe anything. Maybe he went up the side of the house with his bare hands! No matter how he did it, my job was to get him down – before Mum got home from work in an hour's time.

I supposed Mum would prefer it if Josh didn't get hurt in the process. At the moment, I didn't much care. At least Josh is quiet when he cries. He's the only kid I know who cries silent tears. Maybe that's supposed to make up for all the racket he creates in the rest of his waking hours.

"Josh, you'd better get down. You could hurt yourself," I yelled up.

"No I won't, Katie," he yelled back. "I'm made of feathers and steel."

"You are not," I yelled back. "You're made of blood and guts, and if you don't get down here now, they'll be spattered all over."

Josh made wings with his hands at the side of his head and stuck out his tongue at me.

It was going to be a long hour, I could tell.

I went into the kitchen and made a sandwich. I could hear

Josh clumping around on the roof above me. Suddenly, I got an idea. I layered a thick slice of bread with peanut butter, then smothered it about an inch thick with jam, put the whole mess on a plate and put it outside where Josh could see it. I didn't say anything, just went back into the kitchen and waited. A few minutes later, Josh stumbled in at the door, smearing it with sticky jam on the way.

I marched him to the bathroom for a clean-up and turned on the TV. Josh flopped down on a pillow about three feet from the screen, put his thumb in his mouth, curled his first finger round

his nose – and watched. It was his quiet position. I think it's a little silly that Josh still sucks his thumb, but at least he is quiet while he does it. Maybe this quiet would last until Mum got home.

I wonder how Josh beats me home from school every day. We both go to Hawthorne Junior. (Josh is a first-year and I'm in the fourth.) We both come out of school at half-past three, but Josh beats me home every time. I don't run, but I'm a fast walker. I think Josh must come out of that school door like a bullet from a gun. He's still ricocheting off the walls by the time I catch up with him at home.

Carolyn Nystrom

What's wrong with Josh?

Josh is hyperactive. Hyperactive children want to be on the move all the time. They find it hard to sit still, even for a moment, and concentrate on things. This makes it difficult for them to learn, too.

As babies, they are very restless. They seem to need a lot less sleep than other babies, and often cry a lot. They may take longer to talk. But they can certainly make loud noises!

Walking and running are sometimes harder for hyperactive children. They may be more clumsy than other children, and trip over things, fall down and get hurt more often. Even at night they find it difficult to slow down. They don't sleep as long as other children. And they often wake up in the night.

School is especially difficult. It's hard to sit still and be quiet when you want to jump and run and shout.

No one is sure why some children are hyperactive and others are not.

The Trouble With Josh

PSHE and citizenship learning objectives

◆ To understand that there are different kinds of responsibilities, rights and duties at home, at school and in the community, and that these can sometimes conflict with each other (2d).

◆ To learn that differences and similarities between people arise from a number of factors, including disability (4f).

◆ To know where individuals families and groups can get help and support (4g).

Background notes

This text focuses on a child who is hyperactive – he has Attention Deficit Hyperactivity Disorder and, therefore, special educational needs. The discussion arising from this text can be used as a starting point to discuss other special needs. You may need to deal very sensitively with this and confirm that any children like this in school are different but no less important and deserve equal status.

Vocabulary

Disability, hyperactive, responsible, ricocheting, danger.

Discussing the text

◆ The text is split into two sections. It is mainly a narrative tale about Josh, but includes an explanation about hyperactivity (ADHD) and how it affects individuals, which puts the behaviour of Josh into context. Read the whole extract together, then ask the children if their opinions about Josh's behaviour changed as they listened. Why? What information did they have by the end of the text? What did they think about Josh at first?

◆ What relationship is Katie to Josh? How old are they? What do the children think Katie feels about having to look after her brother?

◆ Ask the children to describe Josh's *quiet position*. Do any of the children in the class have certain positions they adopt when they are being quiet and still? How does being like this make them feel? How might Josh feel when he is in his quiet position?

◆ Discuss the strong visual image of Josh *ricocheting off the walls*, and make sure all the children understand what *ricocheting* means. Talk about what is meant by the term *hyperactive* and explain that there are different types of hyperactivity, some worse than others. Explain that some children like Josh have to have medicine each day to help them control what they do. On this day in the story, Josh had forgotten to have his medicine at school and so he was excessively lively. What dangers did he put himself in? What other side effects of his hyperactivity are discussed in the text? How might these things affect his everyday life? (For example, in school, he may not have friends because other children don't understand his behaviour or they don't want to sit next to him because he distracts them and gets them into trouble.)

◆ You may have a child in your class who is hyperactive. If so, deal sensitively with this, but it may be appropriate for him or her, with the support of peers, to explain about the impact the condition has on his life and how he feels about not being able to concentrate. Does he deliberately do things that are disruptive, wrong or dangerous? This may help others in the class to be more understanding and tolerant of his behaviour.

PSHE and citizenship activities

◆ Talk about how we often judge people without knowing what they are like, what experiences they have had, or if they have an illness or disability that isn't immediately apparent. Stress that we should get to know someone a little bit before we make judgements about them.

◆ Discuss with the children different types of disabilities. They may suggest the more obvious ones, such as people in wheelchairs, people who are blind or deaf. Then talk about conditions that may not be as obvious but still affect people's lives. Reinforce the fact that some disabilities don't affect the way people live their everyday lives except that they do certain things differently or have to be careful about what they do (for example, someone who is partially deaf but can use a hearing aid to make out most sounds, or someone with epilepsy), but some do have a profound affect on individuals and their families (such as someone with severe mobility difficulties). It is important to emphasise that all people need to be loved and respected for who they are, but some people need more care and help than others. Ask the children to use charity websites, such as the RNIB, the National Multiple Sclerosis Society and RADAR to gain information about disabilities and how they affect people's lives.

◆ Ask half the class to focus on Katie, the narrator of the story and to imagine they are her. How would they feel on the day in the story? How would they feel having to be responsible for Josh every day after school? Tell them to write a diary extract for Katie, explaining how she feels about Josh. Then ask the other half of the class to imagine they are Josh and that they are sitting quietly reflecting on what they have been doing. Ask them to write a diary entry for him, describing how he feels, what he finds hard to cope with and how his condition affects his everyday life.

◆ If Josh were in the children's class, what procedures could be put into place to help him? (Perhaps he could have a 'quiet chair' for moments when things gets too much, a friend next to him could help with his work.) Ask the children to work in groups to decide on details for a care guide.

◆ If you have any children with disabilities, you might want to ask them, with partners, to write down how things could be made acceptable for them or what rules they would like put in place. For example, if you have a child in a wheelchair, you may decide as a class not to go on a trip where there isn't suitable access. It is important to stress in this activity that we are not feeling sorry for the person, but being fair to them in the way they are catered for.

◆ Although children under 14 shouldn't be left on their own, it does happen. Ask the children to make a booklet of rules and information for keeping safe when in the house on their own. What would they do if there was an emergency? Do the children know which neighbours they could go to? Do they have emergency phone numbers, for example parents' work numbers, friends' numbers and so on? Get the children to ask at home and learn some of these. A similar activity could be done around playing outside and what to do if a crisis happened.

Further literacy ideas

◆ Ask the children to write an imaginary story or a recount about looking after a younger child. When something went wrong, how did they cope? What did they do? How was the problem resolved?

◆ Ask the children to look at their own characteristics and personal likes and dislikes. Tell them to write about these in a positive way in a piece of information text or a poem. Share these with the class so it can be emphasised that we are all different and that makes the world a much more interesting and special place to live.

◆ In groups, ask the children to make a new set of school rules. If they could decide what the rules were, what would they have? Tell them that they can include funny ones, but nothing dangerous. Ask each group to present their choices to the rest of the class.

Let's Talk About Racism

Why talk about racism?

Racist jokes, name-calling and violent racist attacks happen all the time and yet many people try to pretend that racism is not a problem. If you look and listen carefully, you will come across racism every day. Racism means that some people make judgements about you without bothering to find out what you are like. Some people get treated unfairly because of racism. Racism deepens misunderstanding between groups of people who could learn from each other and live together. There are thousands of racist attacks in Britain every year. Many families live in fear because of threats to them and their homes.

What is racism?

We all belong to one race, the human race. But everyone is different. We are all individuals. You are not the same as your mother or father, brothers or sisters, although you may look like them. Your whole personality and body are all your own. You may look more like some people in your class than others, but that does not mean you are similar to them. Your best friend may have another religion or speak another first language from you.

Racism is the mistaken belief that there are distinct groups, or races, within the human race, with particular characteristics which affect how they behave. People with these ideas think 'their' race is better than others. The views of those around them and some books, newspapers and films may have misled them into thinking in this way. Scientists have been unable to discover ways of separating the human race into distinct races.

Racism occurs when you distance yourself from someone else because you think they come from a different place or kind of people. You decide that they do not belong to your group. You do this because of a person's colour or the way they talk or sometimes their religion.

As a result of racism some groups in our society have more power and status than others. Racial discrimination – which means giving houses, jobs or educational opportunities on the grounds of race – is against the law in Britain. But racial abuse happens in many places: on the bus, in the playground, and even in the classroom. Although people can take cases of racial abuse to court, it can be very difficult to prove what exactly happened. However, when someone wins a case of racial discrimination, it shows that people are willing to work for a fairer society.

It takes courage to find out what a person is really like if friends or parents are telling you not to. Michael and Ngugi are in the same class. Michael said, "I don't play with Africans." This is racism. The two boys support the same football team, like the same music, share the same favourite foods. If Michael had asked Ngugi about himself, he would have found this out. They have more in common than Michael and his cousin. But Michael was prejudiced against Ngugi without even speaking to him.

Angela Grunsell

Let's Talk About Racism

Display photographs, pictures and books showing different races and differences that occur through culture and religion. Also, collect newspaper articles about racist attacks.

PSHE and citizenship learning objectives

◆ To recognise their worth as individuals (1b).

◆ To research, discuss and debate topical issues, problems and events (2a).

◆ To understand that there are different kinds of responsibilities, rights and duties at home, at school and in the community, and that these can sometimes conflict with each other (2d).

◆ To appreciate the range of national, regional, religious and ethnic identities in the UK (2i).

◆ To realise the nature and consequences of racism, teasing and bullying, and how to respond to them and ask for help (4d).

◆ To appreciate that differences and similarities between people arise from a number of factors, including cultural, ethnic, racial and religious diversity (4f).

Background notes

Racism can be defined as a deliberate denigration of a particular race or culture based on irrational judgements of worth, resulting in stereotyping with hostile or negative attitudes towards that culture or race. It is therefore a very emotive subject to discuss with children. However, it is vitally important to raise their awareness of how hurtful and damaging and misguided racist comments can be and to reinforce that we are all equal and all important, no matter what our colour or creed. It is especially important to address this topic in a monocultural classroom.

Vocabulary

Race, racist, cultural, religious, prejudice, values, beliefs, individual, identity, respect.

Discussing the text

◆ Read the text through with the children. Where does the term *racism* come from? Look at the word *race* and explain what it means. Briefly discuss the origins of different races from a historical perspective. Before we had movement around the world people lived in one place and were closely related to people who lived near them and looked like them. Therefore, in various parts of the world, we had particular physical traits. Gradually, people were able to move around the world more and now we have a multiracial society. With older children, you will be able to look at this with a closer link to geography and history.

◆ Discuss the points made in the text about racism being about a person's colour, the way they talk or their religion. Do the children think it is right to use these categories to label people as all the same? Have any of the children experienced people not wanting to be friends because of these things? How did they feel? Have they ever judged people along these lines? Say that sometimes people do this because they don't understand that everyone is different and they may be unsettled by the way people look or act because they are not exactly like themselves. Stress that this is not an excuse and we are all responsible for helping people understand that everyone is an individual. We are all different in some ways from everyone else and that makes each of us special. There are good and bad people, irrespective of colour, religion, country of origin or the way they speak.

◆ Examine the case of the two boys in the text. What do the children think about Michael's attitude? How do they think Ngugi feels about Michael's comments? Discuss the word *prejudice* and explain that sometimes we are prejudiced without thinking and realising what we are doing, and this may be linked to values we have learned at home or from our friends.

PSHE and citizenship activities

◆ The text illustrates a need to discuss racism with children and to focus on what it is. It is important to help children realise that racism is a real problem, even though some people like to think it doesn't exist. Look at news articles about racist attacks or conflicts. Carefully share these and discuss what is happening in the stories. Then discuss why we need to talk about racism. Has anyone in the class been called names because of the way they look, for example their clothing or the colour of their skin? How did this make them feel? Generate a discussion that these things do not make someone better or worse than others and that everyone is an individual, different from everyone else.

◆ Focus on physical appearances and get the children to look at differences of skin colour, skin tone, hair colour, hair type, eye shape, nose shape and so on. Ask them in pairs to use a mirror to see differences between themselves, using the head area only. Ask them to report these findings to the rest of the class. Were any two heads identical? What were the major areas of difference? Still in pairs, ask the children to draw a portrait of their partner using pastels and paint. Ask them to work hard on colour matching. Display all the class portraits and this should emphasise the great diversity. Children could write about their partner's looks to go alongside these.

◆ Now look at personality traits. Working in the same pairs, ask the children to talk about what they like doing, what hobbies they have, whether they are moody, lively and so on. Again, share all the information. You may like to make some graphs of the results, showing, for example, how many children like football, watching cartoons, reading, drawing and so on.

◆ These activities should help children to realise that each of us is different and we should not be labelled. Ask individuals to write about what they have learned from exploring the information.

◆ Ask about the religious beliefs in your class. Which religions do the children feel they belong to? Why? Who goes to a place of worship regularly? What is it? (Synagogue, mosque, church and so on.) Encourage children from a variety of religions to talk about what they believe and how they worship. If the school is in a predominantly Christian area, use textbooks or schools television programmes to explore other religions. Encourage children to respect different beliefs, just as they should respect people who like doing different things from themselves.

◆ Look at the range of cultural differences within the class. Ask the children to write about the traditions that they have. Some of these will be purely family-based and some from religion. Share some of the children's writing and discuss the similarities and differences between families, highlighting the similar things that families do and reinforcing the fact that the variety is also of benefit to society.

◆ Ask the children to write a letter to Michael explaining that he is being racist and describing how hurt and upset he is making Ngugi feel. Tell them to include advice about what he should do (for example, apologise and get to know Ngugi) and how he might find they have a lot in common.

◆ Ask the children to write a piece of instructional text about how not to be prejudiced.

Further literacy ideas

◆ Ask the children to write their own story in which someone is prejudiced or racist and how, in the end, they come to realise that they are wrong.

◆ Look at generic features and help the children to write their own explanation texts about racism.

◆ Examine the construction of the word *prejudice*, and investigate more words beginning with *pre*.

CHAPTER 3

Developing self-esteem

During Key Stage 2, a large part of children's development is linked to becoming independent, confident young people. Children begin to make important decisions for themselves and are often responsible for their own actions. To have the confidence to say *No* to peers, or to adults, in situations that they are unsure of means that children need to have a well-developed sense of positive self-esteem. Self-esteem often needs specifically developing with individuals to enable them to value a wide variety of things within themselves and to help them become aware that the stereotypical images of what is good or successful are not always the only ones or the right ones. Those children who are less able academically or less capable in sport often feel badly about themselves because achievement in these areas is what society tends to value. The extracts chosen for this chapter work on developing a sense of identity with individuals and of valuing a wide range of attributes, from being kind and thoughtful to being very good at one particular subject.

All children make judgements about themselves and others and children have a tendency to fall out and be cruel to each other. This is never going to stop – it is part of growing up, but we can help individuals to cope with these situations in a positive way and to be minimally affected by them. When working on building self-esteem, some children may get too confident and cocky and this must also be avoided, so, although we encourage individuals to know their strengths, we also try to help them acknowledge their weaknesses and set goals for improving them.

I know someone

Genre
humorous
poem with
refrain

I know someone who can
take a mouthful of custard and blow it
down their nose.
I know someone who can
make their ears wiggle.
I know someone who can
shake their cheeks so it sounds
like ducks quacking.
I know someone who can
throw peanuts in the air and catch them
in their mouth.
I know someone who can
balance a pile of 12 2p pieces on his elbow
and snatch his elbow from under them
and catch them.
I know someone who can
bend her thumb back to touch her wrist.
I know someone who can
crack his nose.
I know someone who can
say the alphabet backwards.
I know someone who can put their hands in
their armpits and blow raspberries.
I know someone who can
wiggle her little toe.
I know someone who can
lick the bottom of her chin.
I know someone who can
slide their top lip one way
and their bottom lip the other way.
and that someone is
ME.

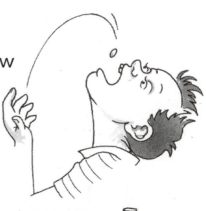

Michael Rosen

I know someone

Display pictures or photographs of children in the class and their own poems they write in the style of Michael Rosen's poem 'I know someone'.

PSHE and citizenship learning objectives

◆ To recognise their worth as individuals by identifying positive things about themselves and their achievements (1b).
◆ To appreciate the range of national, regional, religious and ethnic identities in the UK (2i).
◆ To be aware of different types of relationship and develop the skills to be effective in relationships (4c).
◆ To recognise and challenge stereotypes (4e).

Vocabulary
Myself, difference, special, achievement, unique, skills, strengths.

Discussing the text
◆ Read the poem to the children twice. Encourage them the first time to just listen and then, on the second hearing, to mimic the actions.
◆ Ask for volunteers to demonstrate or tell the class about something they can do that makes them special or different.
◆ What do the children notice about the style and layout of the poem? (For example, its repeating line, no verse breaks, the illustration.)
◆ Discuss why the children think Michael Rosen wrote this poem and how he felt when he wrote it. Do they think he was like the child in the poem? If so, why?
◆ Talk about what makes us all special, how individual differences should be valued and that the differences make our world a rich place to live.
◆ Get the children to think about what they can do that is special, helps others or makes life better for other people, for example be kind to people, ask how they feel, send caring notes, help to tidy up.
◆ What makes a good friend? Ask the children to think about a good friend and describe what it is that makes him or her good and special. (Perhaps sharing snacks, being invited to his or her house, playing together.)

PSHE and citizenship activities
◆ Ask the children to write a poem about themselves using the style of Michael Rosen: *I know someone who can…* Remind them to focus on positive achievements. Referring to the poem, help the children to understand that even the little skills and idiosyncrasies they have, that may not seem particularly important or useful, contribute to making them different and special. More confident children should be able to write a longer poem, but you may want to support less able children with

a sheet with the repeated line printed on it. Collect all the poems together to make a class book, decorated with drawings and photographs of the children.

◆ If possible, organise the children into friendship pairs to discuss the qualities of the friendship and then write a piece beginning, for example *Joanne is a good friend because…*

◆ Ask the children to consider and make notes on the different roles that they have in their lives. What qualities do they need to be good at these? For example, *I am a good son because I help my dad wash up, I am a good friend because I listen to my friend when she is sad.*

◆ Ask the children to draw a large outline of themselves and write inside it the qualities which make them special to other people. They could also do the same for their friends.

◆ Individually, help the children to design a personal shield or coat of arms to show four competencies or strengths of personality that they have.

◆ Ask the children to make posters or collages using photographs and headlines from magazines, drawings and so on of what they are good at doing, the hobbies that they enjoy.

◆ In pairs, ask the children to discuss and make lists of positive and qualities they like in other people. Tell them to consider their parents and famous people as well as their friends.

◆ The children could make passports of themselves and write a personal statement inside describing their looks and character.

Further literacy ideas

◆ Use the poem as a model for a repeating line poem for other topics, for example *I know a hand that can… I know a friend that can… I know a mum that can…*

◆ The children could write a character profile for a teacher in their school, or a classmate, using a variety of adjectives.

◆ In pairs, ask the children to choose a character from a story they have recently read. Tell them to write a character profile, using evidence from the text to support their comments.

◆ Look at other poems by Michael Rosen. Discuss the styles, structures and humour of his poetry.

◆ Set the children a task to find out as much as they can about Michael Rosen as an author, using blurbs from books, and Internet sources. They could even write to publishers for biographical and bibliographical information.

◆ Together, make a list of all the verbs in the text. Ask the children to add adverbs into each sentence. Then make a list of nouns from the text, adding adjectives into each sentence.

The Balaclava story

Genre
*longer
narrative
fiction*

Tony and Barry both had one. I reckon half the kids in our class had one. But I didn't. My mum wouldn't even listen to me.

"You're not having a balaclava! What do you want a balaclava for in the middle of summer?"

I must've told her about ten times why I wanted a balaclava.

"I want one so's I can join the Balaclava Boys…"

"Go and wash your hands for tea, and don't be so silly."

She turned away from me to lay the table, so I put the curse of the middle finger on her. This was pointing both your middle fingers at somebody when they weren't looking. Tony had started it when Miss Taylor gave him a hundred lines for flicking paper pellets at Jennifer Greenwood. He had to write out a hundred times: "I must not fire missiles because it is dangerous and liable to cause damage to someone's eye."

Tony tried to tell Miss Taylor that he hadn't fired a missile, he'd just flicked a paper pellet, but she threw a piece of chalk at him and told him to shut up.

"Don't just stand there – wash your hands."

"Eh?"

"Don't say 'eh', say 'pardon'."

"What?"

"Just hurry up, and make sure the dirt comes off in the water, and not on the towel, do you hear?"

Ooh, my mum. She didn't half go on sometimes.

"I don't know what you get up to at school. How do you get so dirty?"

I knew exactly the kind of balaclava I wanted. One just like Tony's, a sort of yellowy-brown. His dad had given it to him because of his earache. Mind you, he didn't like wearing it at first. At school he'd given it to Barry to wear and got it back before home-time. But, all the other lads started asking if they could have a wear of it, so Tony took it back and said from then on nobody but him could wear it, not even Barry. Barry told him he wasn't bothered because he was going to get a balaclava of his own, and so did some of the other lads. And that's how it started – the Balaclava Boys.

It wasn't a gang really. I mean they didn't have meetings or anything like that. They just went around together wearing their balaclavas, and if you didn't have one you couldn't go around with them. Tony and Barry were my best friends, but because I didn't have a balaclava, they wouldn't let me go round with them. I tried.

"Aw, go on, Barry, let us walk round with you."

"No, you can't. You're not a Balaclava Boy."

"Aw, go on."

"No."

"Please."

I don't know why I wanted to walk round with them anyway. All they did was wander up and down the playground dressed in their rotten balaclavas. It was daft.

"Go on, Barry, be a sport."

"I've told you. You're not a Balaclava Boy. You've got to have a balaclava. If you get one, you can join."

"But I can't, Barry. My mum won't let me have one."

"Hard luck."

"You're rotten."

Then he went off with the others. I wasn't half fed up. All my friends were in the Balaclava Boys. All the lads in my class except me. Wasn't fair. The bell went for the next lesson – ooh heck, handicraft with the Miseryguts Garnett – then it was home-time. All the Balaclava Boys were going in and I followed them.

"Hey, Tony, do you want to go down the woods after school?"

"No, I'm going round with the Balaclava Boys."

"Oh."

Blooming Balaclava Boys. Why wouldn't *my mum* buy *me* a *balaclava*? Didn't she realise that I was losing all my friends, and just because she wouldn't buy me one?

"Eh, Tony, we can go goose-gogging – you know, by those great gooseberry bushes at the other end of the woods."

"I've told you, I can't."

"Yes, I know, but I thought you might want to go goose-gogging."

"Well, I would, but I can't."

I wondered if Barry would be going as well.

"Is Barry going round with the Balaclava Boys an' all?"

"Course he is."

"Oh."

Blooming balaclavas. I wish they'd never been invented.

George Layton

The Balaclava story

Display a balaclava and a variety of popular artefacts of the moment, such as designer trainers, a logo T-shirt, the current 'in' toy.

PSHE and citizenship learning objectives

◆ To recognise their worth as individuals by identifying positive things about themselves and their achievements (1b).

◆ To know how to look after their money and realise that future wants and needs may be met through saving (1f).

◆ To realise the consequences of anti-social and aggressive behaviour on individuals (2c).

◆ To appreciate that resources can be allocated in different ways and that these economic choices affect individuals and communities (2j).

◆ To recognise and challenge stereotypes (4e).

Vocabulary

Balaclava, goose-gogging, self-esteem, trends, ringleader, gang.

Discussing the text

◆ Read the whole text with the children. Ask the children in pairs to quickly discuss how they would summarise the content of the extract, then report these summaries back to the class. Discussion here should focus on the fact that the main character in the story wants to be just like his friend and he can't be.

◆ Ask the children what a balaclava is. If you have one, or a picture of one, let them look at it. What do they think of it? Would they want to wear one?

◆ Look at the *curse of the middle finger* in the extract. What do the children think this is? Will it really do any harm? Why did Tony use it? Focus on this helping Tony feel better about being told off. Do the children do anything like this? When? Who to?

◆ What sort of character do we think Tony is from the information in the text? Look at the idea of a ringleader – someone who initiates and whom others always follow. Is this good? Should we always copy the leader?

◆ Do the children know what *goose-gogging* is? (Picking gooseberries.)

◆ Discuss why the main character in the story didn't feel like the rest of his friends. Have any of the children in the class felt like this? Ask them to share their experiences.

◆ Ask the children what they think about the way Tony and Barry treated the narrator. Have they ever done this to someone? How do they feel about that now? Can they suggest what Tony and Barry could have done to make the boy in the story feel better? (They could have let him join in even without a balaclava or they could have shared it with him.) What could the children learn from this story? Draw out that genuine friendship is more than wearing a balaclava! Look at Tony's response *'Well, I would, but I can't.'* Why did he say this? Explore how he may have wanted to spend time with the narrator but felt the pressure of being part of the group.

◆ Discuss why the boy can't have a balaclava. Find the evidence in the text. Do the children think this is the only or real reason? Have any of them experienced the same sort of conversation with their parents?

PSHE and citizenship activities

◆ Discuss whether the children think Mum is being fair or not. Ask them to write lists of reasons why she is and isn't.

◆ In the story, the boys are all wearing balaclavas. What trends are the children aware of in their class or in school, for example a certain brand of trainers, the new playground game pieces, collecting the latest cartoon-related picture cards or figures and so on? Get the children to make a list of trendy 'must-haves', looking at last year and this year and how these trends change. How many children in the class had or didn't have them? What has happened to the things that are no longer fashionable or trendy? Discuss how the boy in the story feels about being left out. Revisit the idea of feeling good or bad about yourself. What experiences can the children share that make them feel good or bad? Ask the children to choose one of the things that makes them feel bad about themselves, then ask a partner to help them decide what they could do about this. For example, if they feel bad that people don't like sitting next to them, they could look at why people don't like to sit next to them – perhaps they kick or swing their feet. They could try to stop kicking people and tell everyone they are trying really hard do this and would like reminding if they lapse. Ask the children to list what they will try to do and, together, agree targets for a period of time, such as a week. Award certificates for completion, and encourage them to continue.

◆ Consider whether or not all the trendy artefacts are value for money. Do the children think any are expensive? Have any of their parents said they can't have something all their friends have got because it is too expensive or they don't have enough money to spend on something like that this week. What does this mean? Where do parents get their money? Try to help children realise that money is not easily come by and is available in a limited supply. Discuss the saying *money doesn't grow on trees*. Have any of their parents used this expression?

◆ Try to help children understand that different people have different amounts of money to spend and therefore have to decide carefully how to spend it. Use the idea of saving up pocket money and having to decide what to buy with it because we can't have all the things we want. To reinforce this point, you could make an activity worksheet in which the children have various amounts of money and a selection of objects to buy. They will need to decide what they can afford to buy and what they should prioritise, for example one expensive thing or a few things that are less expensive or nothing and save up for next week.

Further literacy ideas

◆ Ask the children to make a mini-dictionary of slang words and sayings that they use, for example *cool*, *sad* and *wicked*, with the meanings alongside them.

◆ Look at the speech within the extract and investigate the use of punctuation and speech marks. For example, when a question is asked, where does the question mark go? Ask the children to write a conversation between the narrator and his mum in which he is explaining why he wants a balaclava.

◆ See if the children can finish off the story, explaining what happens to the boy. Does he get a balaclava? How? Or does a new trend get started by him? Does he make some new friends?

◆ Ask the children to write a diary extract for the boy for a few days. Encourage them to explore what happens and how he feels.

◆ Ask them to write an extract from Mum's point of view, explaining why she doesn't want her son to have a balaclava.

The king's daughter

Genre
historical fiction, diary extract

January 7 (the 15th year of my father's reign)

Why is it always me who gets into trouble? I couldn't help it.

I was so looking forward to the feast last night and it was wonderful at first. The Hall was full. Father and Mother looked magnificent and even the wolfhounds had been washed and brushed. They sat at Father's feet all night.

Father was seated at the top table with my older brother Edward on one side and my eldest sister Fleese on the other. It was a great honour for her to be on the top table. She's 17 now and I think she's Father's favourite. He lets her do almost anything!

Mother sat at the side table with my sister Giffy, my brother Waldo and me. Once she had served Father his wine, she stayed with us.

I was allowed to eat anything I liked. I had to stop after the third plateful because I felt sick.

The smoke from the torches made my eyes sting and I got very hot. There was lots of noise and I asked Mother if I could go to bed but she said "No," I would have to wait for Father to dismiss us.

The food was cleared at last, but before Mother could ask if we could go to bed, Father told Waldo to come up to the dais and recite a poem for everyone. He's only seven but he already reads Saxon better than I do. He loved every moment of it. He recited by heart, not just one but three poems and they were very, very long ones! Everyone clapped and cheered when he had finished and Father gave him a present for being so clever. It was a book.

Waldo was so pleased with himself that I couldn't help myself. As he walked past, I stuck my foot out. He went flying and landed flat on his face on the dirty rushes, then he burst into tears. I laughed. No one else did.

There was a scary silence. Mother started forward but Father stopped her. He came down himself and picked Waldo up. For a moment, Father stared at me and I started to shake. I was frightened he would shout at me but he turned to Waldo and told him about the time that Alexander the Great had fallen over when he was conquering somewhere. Father made everyone laugh with the story. Then he let Mother take Waldo off to bed and told Edith, our nurse, to take Giffy and me away too.

I wish I hadn't tripped Waldo up. Father knows it was me. He knows everything.

Gillian Goddard

The king's daughter

Display a variety of diary texts, showing the children how a diary is laid out. Include whole texts and annotated copies of extracts, showing the characteristics of the genre.

PSHE and citizenship learning objectives

◆ To recognise their worth as individuals by identifying positive things about themselves and their achievements, seeing their mistakes, making amends and setting personal goals (1b).

◆ To realise the consequences of anti-social and aggressive behaviours on others (2c).

◆ To think about the lives of people living in other places and times, and people with different values and customs (4b).

Background notes

This story is set in Winchester in Wessex in the reign of King Alfred (AD871-899). Alfred reigned at a time of tremendous unrest and fighting. He kept the Vikings from taking over all of England, and he started a system of education, encouraging everyone to learn to read and write. He revised the laws of the kingdom and demanded high standards of justice from his officers. He was a truly great leader. Alfred married a Mercian princess called Elswitha when he was 19 years old. He had five surviving children. The oldest was Aethelflaed (Fleese in the story), then Edward, then Ethelgifu (Giffy), then Elfthryth (Elfrith) and last Ethelweard (Waldo).

This is an extract from the fictional diary of Elfrith, in which she describes and evening when her jealousy gets the better of her.

Vocabulary

Wine, dais, recite, rushes, feast, label, motive, jealousy, proud.

Discussing the text

◆ Put the extract in context (see Background notes above). Explain how long ago this event happened and how, although this is a *fictional* diary extract, it is based on real evidence from historical sources. Read the extract together, then go through it in more detail, making sure that the children understand the historical context. What evidence is there in the text to help us to understand how people lived this long ago?

◆ Look at the opening statement. What does this tell us about how Elfrith thinks about herself? Is there anyone in the class who sometimes feels like this? Ask them to think about what other things happen to them in a negative way, for example they are always the last to finish or it always seem to be them who gets picked last to play football. Discuss with the class how and why individuals get labelled as a slow coach or no good at football and so on.

◆ Discuss why Elfrith did what she did. What evidence is there in the text of how she was feeling? (She was tired and wanted to go to bed, she was jealous of Waldo, she thought he was smug.) Do the children think she was right to do what she did? Can they understand her motives? Do they think she planned it or did it just happen on the spur of the moment? Have any of them just found themselves doing something they regretted straight away?

◆ What does Elfrith think her father's view of her is at the end of the day? Do they think he will be cross with her? Do they think this incident will change how much her father loves her?

PSHE and citizenship activities

◆ Focus on the idea of Elfrith worrying about what her father will think of her. Ask the children what happens to them at home when they are told off. Do they think it stops their parents loving them? Reassure the children that although adults get angry, this does not mean they stop caring about the people they are angry with. Help them to appreciate that, in fact, we tend to get most cross with the people we care about the most because we want the best for them.

◆ Elfrith doesn't think she is a good reader. Ask the children to think of one or two things they aren't particularly good at – perhaps playing the violin or swimming. Look at the range of ideas produced and reinforce the fact that everyone has different things they are good and bad at. For each example, ask the children to make an action plan of what the person could do to improve in that area. (Practise, for example.) Help the children to understand that they might never find this particular thing easy or be the best at it, but they can increase their own standard.

◆ Tell the children that although Elfrith is not a good reader we learn later in the story that she plays the harp really well. Ask children to write about something they do well, listing what it takes to be good at it. Reinforce that the things we are good at do not need to be school related. For example, being sensitive and kind is something to be proud of, and not everyone can do it well.

◆ Prepare a celebration assembly to share with the school all the things that your class members are good at. Use this opportunity to emphasise the range of activities, for example skipping, maths, tidying-up, reading, listening to friends, helping parents with housework, and so on.

◆ In diary form, ask the children to write about something they have done and regretted. What caused their action? How did they feel afterwards? Did they resolve the situation?

◆ Ask the children to think of reasons that the king's family may be celebrating and then to write about a celebration they have been to. What was it for? Who else was there? What form did it take? What did people wear? Was there music?

Further literacy ideas

◆ Ask the children to keep a diary in class for a week. What sorts of things are written in diaries? Look at a range of diary texts for example, Anne Frank's, Sue Townsend's *Adrian Mole* books and *The Country Diary of an Edwardian Lady* by Edith Holden.

◆ Ask the children to write about their fathers or a significant male in their lives, describing what they look like, their non-physical characteristics, what they like doing together and so on. Be sensitive to those who don't have contact with a father and encourage them to choose a stepdad or grandad, uncle or male friend of the family.

◆ Investigate the combination of tenses we use when writing diaries. Why is the last little bit written differently from the rest of the text? Discuss that in diaries we write about things that have happened, how we feel now and about things that may happen in the future. Together, try writing about one event in the past, present and future. Then set the children to work individually on writing a diary entry based around that event.

◆ Ask the children to write an acrostic poem for *celebration*, focusing on things that they are good at and like doing.

Crying to get out

Inside every fat girl
There's a thin girl crying to get out
Sweet and sad and slinky
That nobody ever knows about

Inside every old man
There's a young man crying to get out
Just behind the wrinkles
Is the kid who used to twist and shout

It's the envelope that lies
Only look into their eyes
See the lonely dreamers there
Building castles in the air

Inside every hater
There's a lover dying of the drought
Inside every killer
There's a lover crying to get out
Trying to get out
Dying to get out
All the locked up lovers
Crying to get out

Fran Landesman

Genre
rhythmic
poetry with
an ABCB
rhyming
pattern

Crying to get out

Display photographs or illustrations of people presented in a stereotypical way, for example a fat woman, an evil-looking man, a sad child, an old granny and so on.

PSHE and citizenship learning objectives

◆ To know about the range of jobs carried out by people they know, and to understand how they can develop skills to make their own contribution in the future (1e).
◆ To explore how the media present information (2k).
◆ To think about the lives of people living in other places and people with different values (4b).
◆ To recognise and challenge stereotypes (4e).
◆ To know where individuals, families and groups can get help and support (4g).

Background notes

This is a difficult text in parts, so if using it with Years 3 and 4, perhaps consider using just the first two verse and corresponding activities. Year 6 children should be able to cope with the whole text.

Vocabulary

Stereotypes, unhappy, media, characters, appearance, personality, image, positive.

Discussing the text

◆ Decide whether you are going to use only the first two verses or the whole text, depending on the children you are working with. Focus initially on verses one and two. Read these with the children and discuss what messages the poet is telling us. Look at the idea of outward appearances not always being an accurate indication of what people are really like, and that we don't always look how we

would want to. Discuss the two 'every' characters in detail and why they look the way they do. Do they feel that they have any control over how they look or how others see them? Do they have any control over how they behave or portray themselves to everyone else?

◆ If using verses three and four, continue this discussion, using the text as extra evidence. What is *the envelope*? (The outer cover – our bodies – that tells us nothing about what goes on inside.) Help the children to realise that for some people (*the lonely dreamers… building castles in the air*), their dreams and ideas of how life should be are inaccessible and unachievable. Discuss how they might be able to move on and help themselves feel better.

PSHE and citizenship activities

◆ What overall feelings does the poem leave us with? Why? Discuss disappointment and sadness linked to empathy for those people who are not as they would like to be. Remind the children that life is what you make it and you *can* have control and help yourself to be happy. Often, people strive to be like media images and this is not possible, nor preferable really, for most people. Emphasise that just because the media present a particular image, shape, size or 'look' as positive or negative, it doesn't mean that we should see it that way. What do we need in our lives to make us happy? Look at the idea of family, a home, friends helping to make our lives good. Ask the children to write about what makes them happy. This could also include their pets, their favourite possessions, their leisure interests and so on.

◆ Ask the children to write about what they would want their lives to be like when they grow up. What job would they like to have? Where would they like to live? What would they like to do as hobbies and so on?

◆ Set up a class debate about media presentation of images linked to lifestyle and body image. Collect a variety of advertisements and other images from magazines. For each advert, divide a number of children into two groups: one for the advert in terms of its presentation of people, and one against it. Ask them all to develop an argument for persuading the class to have their point of view about whether the advert is good or bad, right or wrong. Then ask the groups to present their arguments to the class. For each advert, have a concluding vote for or against.

◆ Ask the children to write about a friend, using information only a close friend would know. Advise them that it should be something special, based on their experience of the person, and that someone else wouldn't be able to tell from the person's external features.

Further literacy ideas

◆ Look at opposites with the children. Start by using the examples from the text (*fat/thin*, *old/young* and so on) and expand the list. Try to focus on things linked to people's appearance and physical characteristics.

◆ Ask the children to write a story about someone who is judged by their appearance, but in the end turns out to be a very different person from how the other people saw him or her.

◆ Ask the children to write a poem in a similar style to the first two verses of 'Crying to get out', using characteristics that children may exhibit. For example, *Inside every… chatty girl, aggressive girl, kicking boy* and so on.

Genre
explanation

What is shyness?

Shyness is how you feel when you are put in situations when you don't want to say or do anything or even have anybody look at you. You may be visiting a new place or meeting new people; you may be asked to do something you haven't done before. Whatever it is, if you are shy it makes you feel really uncomfortable.

We all have times when we are quiet and don't know what to say to people, or we have to do things that we don't want to do, but shyness is more than this. It is being too scared and nervous to talk to people even if you want to, being unable to join in even if something looks really good fun.

With shyness often comes that embarrassing feeling of blushing the minute someone looks at you or says your name, when you feel your face go all hot and on fire and if you looked in a mirror, you would be all red! You may even feel sick or that you're going to burst into tears. Have you ever felt like this? That's shyness.

Being shy can be hard to cope with. It can get us into trouble because people think we are being rude. Being shy can be hard to live with.

Jackie Barbera

What is shyness?

Write up the word *shy* and around it, add words describing how the children feel when they are being shy.

PSHE and citizenship learning objectives

◆ To recognise their worth as individuals by identifying positive things about themselves and their achievements (1b).

◆ To face new challenges positively by collecting information, looking for help, making responsible choices, and taking action (1c).

Vocabulary

Shyness, blushing, sensitive, embarrassed, confidence, challenge.

Discussing the text

◆ Read the text through with the children. In places, many of them will sympathise with the text. Some may even blush as they recognise themselves. Be careful not to draw attention to this. Discuss that, in fact, in some situations, many of us can feel this embarrassment and lack of confidence. Can any of the children share situations when they have felt shy? For example, starting a new school, going to Brownies or Guides, being asked a question in assembly.

◆ Find out if any of the children feel themselves blushing at times. How do they know they are blushing? How do other people know? What sorts of things can cause this? What else do they feel?

◆ Are there very shy people in the class? Be sensitive here, as they will be shy about saying so unless there is a lot of trust in the classroom. If the atmosphere is right, encourage those children to describe how shyness makes them feel.

◆ As a class, make a list of things that can make us feel shy.

PSHE and citizenship activities

◆ Explain to the children that although most of us feel shy like this at some point, some people feel like this a lot of the time. Discuss how we can help ourselves when we feel like this. Perhaps by taking deep breaths, taking a friend along to support us, reassuring ourselves that it doesn't matter if we make a mistake, comparing it to a similar situation that we handled well. Help the children to realise that it is only through doing things we don't want to do that we can become more comfortable with them and get over some of our shyness. Go on to talk about how we can support other people when we know they are shy, for example by not laughing or pointing it out when they go red or make a mistake, by encouraging them, by responding positively. Ask the children, in pairs, to write a guide to spotting shyness in other people and how to help them to deal with or overcome it. Remind them to use the text and the list of situations in which people feel shy for ideas.

◆ Discuss with the children that there may be times when we don't want to talk to people, for example if we don't know them, and that this is fine. You could make a link here to keeping safe and not talking to strangers.

◆ Ask the children to make a list of things that have made them blush recently, for example being told they look nice, that they have worked hard, being told off, being asked to say something in front of the whole class or in an assembly.

◆ Help the children to investigate and make notes on why and how we blush, using non-fiction printed texts, CD-ROMs or the Internet. Suggest that they research subject areas such as *my body* and *blood systems*.

Further literacy ideas

◆ Ask the children to write a poem entitled 'Shyness is…'. This could be an acrostic poem or a poem in the form of a list.

◆ Look at the suffix *-ness*. Together, make a list of root words that *-ness* can be added to and ask the children to learn to spell some of these words.

◆ Ask the children to use the information they found during their physical processes investigation to write their own explanations of why we blush. Remind them to try to use a structure and style suitable to the explanation genre, including a brief opening introduction to the subject, points explained in some detail and a concluding statement or two.

◆ Tell the children to write a recount about something that made them feel shy, but that they don't feel shy about any more. What did they do? How did they come to terms with it?

◆ Read 'Glenis' by Alan Ahlberg from *Please Mrs Butler*. Why do the children think Glenis is silent? Link this to the children's ideas about shyness.

◆ Ask the children to write a story about a shy boy or girl and how they overcome their shyness on an important occasion, for example by protecting or sticking up for someone else, contributing to the school play and so on.

Coping with crisis and loss

This chapter addresses issues surrounding challenge, fear, sickness, and loss through divorce, separation and bereavement. The planned discussion and consideration of these things sometimes puts off teachers who, quite rightly, do not want to cause their pupils undue worry, distress or fear. Yet there is an obligation in PSHE to help prepare children for life, including survival through life crises. Part of such a programme, and the activities linked to these texts, is directed towards raising the possibilities of loss, sickness and fear as 'normal parts of life'. However, it also gives children rehearsal time to consider survival strategies, and to realise that these experiences are common, not unique, thus combating much of the isolation experienced by children and adults coping in crisis situations.

Inevitably, these areas are very sensitive and will require a strong working knowledge of the children's family situations when working with the texts. Most children will have been ill and away from school for a week or more, most will also have experienced the loss of a pet or a favourite, special toy. These experiences can be drawn upon and carefully explored. Children in the midst of a parental divorce, however, or who have just lost a sibling or parent or grandparent, or who are seriously ill, are likely to be further hurt by the discussion of these texts. On the other hand, children who have recovered from such events of a year or so back may well appreciate the time and context to order their thoughts and share their feelings. (Children's active involvement in discussion, however, should be optional or you could be facing a very distressed or angry child, struggling to cope with feelings that are released after having been buried for some time.)

Education on death and loss is a controversial area, but literature is one of the best ways of introducing this painful reality of life. It helps children understand other children who may have lost a parent or sibling through separation or death. In addition, fears when talked about can lose their potency. It is therefore worth beginning the work in this area at this key stage..

These texts have been selected for Years 3–4 and Years 5–6. For example, 'Goodbye Max' will work well with Year 3 children when discussing bereavement, Robert Westall's 'The Bombs Fall' is best dealt with at Year 5 or 6 when looking at World War II.

Many of the discussion and activity ideas can be adapted to use with other suitable texts that you may be familiar with already.

I Like to Stay Up

Genre
*Rhyming
poem using
West Indian
dialect*

I like to stay up
and listen
when big people talking
jumbie stories

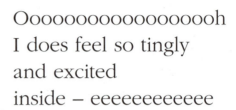

Ooooooooooooooooooh
I does feel so tingly
and excited
inside – eeeeeeeeeeee

But when my mother say
"Girl, time for bed"
then is when
I does feel a dread
then is when
I does jump into me bed
then is when
I does cover up
from me feet to me head

then is when
I does wish
I didn't listen
to no stupid jumbie story
then is when
I does wish
I did read me book instead

Grace Nichols

I Like to Stay Up

Display a picture of a child under his or her bedcovers, with words that describe night-time fear caused by the child's imagination.

PSHE and citizenship learning objectives

◆ To face their fears positively by looking for help, making reasonable choices and taking action (1c).

◆ To know where individuals can get help and support (4g).

◆ To be responsible for their own well-being.

◆ To understand where their fears stem from and use strategies for the management of their fear.

Background notes

This poem introduces the issue of night-time fear. It takes place in a family setting, using West Indian dialect and specific vocabulary, but it addresses a very common problem – that we sometimes enjoy and are excited by stories that then frighten us later in bed in the dark. Learning to avoid scary stories is one solution, coping with fear is another. Both are explored here.

Vocabulary

Fear, scary, frightening, exciting, imagination, nightmare, comfort.

Discussing the text

◆ Discuss the voice and character of the narrator of the poem. Who is speaking? How old is the child and is it a boy or a girl? How can we tell? (The narrator is referred to as *Girl*.)

◆ What do the children think *jumbie* stories are? (Spooky or ghost stories.) Why does the girl like to listen to these? (It makes her feel excited.) Ask the children if they ever like to be frightened a little by exciting but scary stories. If so, why or why not?

◆ Why did the girl regret listening to stories? (When she went to bed, she remembered the stories and they made her really scared.) Have the children ever read, watched or listened to something and then found themselves imagining things from it when they got to bed? Why do they think that happens? (The dark, they're tired and often alone, the images are vivid.) If it comes up in the discussion, talk briefly about nightmares.

◆ Ask the children what they think they should do if they keep imagining scary things in bed at night? (Perhaps wake Mum or Dad; put the light on and read for a while; hold a favourite soft toy; ask Mum or Dad if you can have the landing light on and the door open a little; think of nice things and routine things like what you'll do at school tomorrow.)

◆ Ask the children what someone could do if they have a good imagination that might trouble them at night. (The children might suggest reading a nice story in bed rather than a frightening one; not listening or watching scary things in the evening; having a night light or bedside light that can be put on if you are frightened; keeping a favourite toy close by the bed.)

PSHE and citizenship activities

◆ Ask the children to write a story about a time when they have been frightened at night because they have listened to, read or watched something scary. Encourage them to describe what they did to make themselves less scared so that they could go to sleep.

◆ The children could write poems detailing how they feel when they are frightened. The final verse should describe words that can comfort or help when they are frightened.

◆ In pairs, tell the children to write a series of helpful hints for younger children about getting a good night's sleep. Help them to word-process the hints as a leaflet for a younger class.

◆ Role-play a scene in groups of four showing a little child crying out for his or her brother or sister at night having imagined there are monsters under the bed. Two children play the parents, one the child who is frightened and one the older sibling. Play the scene two ways – the first when the brother or sister either gets cross or ignores the upset child, the second when he or she helps. Then ask each group to play their scenes to the rest of the class. Go on to talk about how we can help our own brothers and sisters, or our friends if they are sleeping over, to overcome their fears.

◆ Discuss with the class why we are more easily frightened at night in the dark. Explain that our feelings are strong because our senses are restricted. Make a point of confirming that monsters do not live under the bed and ghosts or assassins are not going to come out of the wardrobe and hurt them. Encourage the children to think about how they can understand and manage their fears without needing the help of their brothers or sisters or parents.

Further literacy ideas

◆ Identify the words and phrases in the poem that distinguish it as a poem from a specific culture. (For example, *jumbie, I does jump into me bed.*) Together, rewrite a verse of the poem using standard English. Which version do the children prefer? Why?

◆ Look at the use of *Ooooooooooooooooooh* and *eeeeeeeeeeee*. Why did the poet use these non-words? (As phonic words representing sounds we make.) Tell the children to make up some of their own phonic words, recording in writing a sound we make in speech. For example, *Umm, Yuk* and *Ahgh*.

◆ Look at the use of the repeated phrase *then is when*. How is this used to add to the poem's rhythm and flow? In small groups, ask the children to practise reading the poem out loud collectively. Then perform the poem as a class, with different groups reading a verse each. If possible, record the reading then play it back. Re-record it as a choral work for performance or perform it as part of an assembly on fear.

◆ See how many words the children can come up with to describe fear and being frightened. Then ask them to look in thesauruses for a few more.

Shadow of the Minotaur

Genre
Modern
fantasy
including a
version of a
Greek myth

Framed in the half-light of one opening, the beast was pawing the ground.

"I'm not scared."

It wasn't true. What's more, the beast knew. His quavering voice settled on the air, painting a picture of his mounting fear. He was clutching the sword's hilt the way a drowning man clings to a piece of driftwood. For comfort. For survival. And, for the first time, he felt its weight. It made his arm shake. His strength was draining away. He tried to grip the hilt with both hands, steadying his weapon.

"Come on then, what are you waiting for?"

But still the beast stood in the archway, pawing at the floor. It was bigger than a man. It stood almost three metres tall and was massively built with slabs of muscle on its chest and shoulders. Below the waist it was bull-like. It had a swinging tail and mud-splattered hooves. Or was it mud? Above the waist it was a man except, that is, for the head. And what a head! The muzzle was huge and when it opened it revealed the sharp, curved teeth, not of a bull but of a big cat. They were the fangs of a lion or tiger, made for ripping flesh. Its eyes were yellow and blazed unflinchingly through the murk. Then there were the great horns, glinting and sharp, curving from its monstrous brow. Thick and muscular as the neck was, it seemed barely able to support such a fearsome head, and strained visibly under the impossible weight.

"Oh my—"

The beast stepped out from the tunnel, and the boy actually took a few steps back. It was as if his soul had crept out of his body and was tugging at him, begging him to get away. In the sparse light shed from the gratings in the ceiling, the beast looked even more hideous. There was the sweat for a start,

standing out in gleaming beads on that enormous neck and shoulders.

But that wasn't all. The creature was smeared from head to foot with filth and dried blood. It was every inch a killer. The beast began to stamp forward, its hooves clashing on the stone floor. It raised its head, the horns scraping on the ceiling, and gave a bellow that seemed to crush the air.

"I can't do this…"

He fell back, scrambling over obstacles on the floor, and fled. That's when he realised he'd dropped the ball of string. His lifeline had gone.

"Oh no!"

The beast was charging head down.

Got to get out of here!

In his mind's eye, he could see himself impaled on the points of those evil-looking horns, his eyes growing pale and lifeless.

Suddenly, he was running for his life, skidding on the slimy floor.

"Help me!"

He saw the startled brown eyes of the girl above the grating.

"Don't run!" she cried. "Fight. You must fight."

He was almost dying of shame. This wasn't supposed to happen. He wasn't meant to lose and there weren't meant to be witnesses to his defeat.

"Fight," she repeated. "It's the way of things."

The way of things. That's right, he was meant to fight, as a hero. But he couldn't. Not against *that*.

"Please," he begged, turning his face away from the girl in shame, "Somebody help me."

The beast was careering through the tunnels, crashing, bellowing thundering through the maze. Its charge was hot, furious, unstoppable. It was almost on him.

Get me out of here!

"That's it," he cried, throwing down his sword, "I've had enough. Game over!"

Ripping off the mask and gloves, Phoenix bent double gulping down air like it had been rationed. The dank half-light of the tunnels was replaced by the welcome glow from an Anglepoise lamp in his father's study. He glanced at the score bracelet on his wrist. It registered total defeat: **000000**. For a few moments everything was spinning, the claws of the game digging into the flesh of the here and now. Then his surroundings became reassuringly familiar.

He was out.

It **was** *a game!*

"Well?" his dad asked, "What do you think?"

"Mind-blowing," Phoenix panted. "It was all so real. It was like another world. I mean, I *was* Theseus. I went into the palace of the tyrant-king Minos. I could actually touch the stone columns, feel the heat of the braziers, smell the incense."

He knew he was gushing, babbling like a little kid, but he didn't care. "The king's daughter Ariadne helped me and she wasn't just an image on a screen. She was a real girl. Then I actually came face to face with the Minotaur. It was really happening. I believed it." He shivered. "Still do."

"Oh, I could tell how convincing it was," said Dad, enjoying the mixture of excitement and fear in his son's voice. "You were screaming your silly head off by the end. I bet your mother thought I was killing you in here."

Phoenix blushed then, beginning to control his breathing at last, he picked up the mask and gloves and traced the attached wires back to the computer where images of the labyrinth were still flashing away on the screen.

Alan Gibbons

Shadow of the Minotaur

Create a scene from the labyrinth, displaying children's word pictures or favourite words and phrases from the text.

PSHE and citizenship learning objectives

◆ To face new challenges positively by collecting information, looking for help, making responsible choices and taking action (1c).

◆ To recognise the different risks in different situations and then decide how to act responsibly (3e).

◆ To recognise that pressure to behave in a risky way can come from people they know (3f).

◆ To develop the skills to be effective in friendships (4c).

Vocabulary

Fear, frightened, challenge, endurance.

Discussing the text

Read the whole text, observing the reactions of the children. Ask them how they felt when the story was being read, up to *Get me out of here*. Record their words and phrases on a board or flip chart. How did the children feel when the rest of the text was read, particularly at that moment when Phoenix declares *'Game over!'*? Again, note their suggestions.

◆ Why does the story make us feel this way? Is it because of the way it is written, its pace and point of view, the language used or the subject matter? Does the writer deliberately conceal the setting, the fact that the adventure is a game, in order to draw the reader into an exciting start? Discuss each point. The first points are important for literacy understanding; the final one explores the ideas of challenge and fear.

◆ Discuss whether or not the children liked this opening and ask them to justify their reasons. Was it a very clever ploy by the writer? Did they feel tricked? Would they read on? Why?

◆ Why had Phoenix's dad created so scary a computer game? (We like to be excited and frightened. We like to face difficult challenges that test us.) Do the children think it would be popular?

◆ Ask the children if they ever deliberately do things that frighten them, such as reading scary books, telling ghost stories, going on theme park rides. Why do they do this? (We get a buzz, an adrenalin rush, when we experience or sense danger. We get a powerful sense of relief when it is over and we know we are alright and everything is fine.)

◆ Might some children be harmed by this computer game? Allow free responses, but cultivate an awareness that some people might have nightmares or be upset by an experience like this.

◆ Stress that we all respond to frightening situations in different ways. We all find different things frightening. We have to be sensitive to other people's feelings and not tease them if they don't want to join in. Similarly, if we find ourselves getting very frightened by something our friends are doing, we should pull out of the activity and don't mind their teasing.

◆ Ariadne encourages Phoenix/Theseus by saying, 'You must fight… It's the way of things.' Talk about the idea that all of us need to face challenges that push us to our limits – whether facing up to our worst fears, taking part in a competition or running long distances that push us to the limit of our endurance. Give examples of one or two great achievers who have done this, for example Steven Redgrave, Nelson Mandela or Martin Luther King, or give an illustration from your own experience.

P SHE and citizenship activities

◆ In pairs, encourage the children to talk about and note down the things that particularly frighten them and what it is about those things that disturb them so much. Then help them to come up with possible ways of coping with that fear or overcoming it. (These could include avoidance, reasoning, having support from friends, confronting the fear.)

◆ Ask the children to act out a story in which a group of friends get involved in a scary situation. Explain that one child gets really frightened and wants to stop. Tell the children to rehearse the scene showing what happens next before playing it to the class. Use these mini-dramas to show that part of the responsibility of friendship is in not deliberately hurting or upsetting friends – good friends take care of each other and understand that they can have different points of view.

◆ Individually, the children could write a poem about their feelings when on a fast ride or when facing a particular challenge that calls for a great deal of determination from them.

◆ In pairs, ask the children to investigate famous achievers, such as Tanni Grey-Thompson and Stephen Hawking, who have faced great challenges or overcome great difficulties and look at how they did so. Make a display about these achievers, focusing on the positive and inspirational aspects of overcoming challenges.

Further literacy ideas

◆ In groups, see what exciting and scary computer games the children enjoy. Ask them to identify what makes these so thrilling and the sorts of children or adults that would like them. They should then choose one each to write a review and a recommendation guide.

◆ The children could write a word picture for words to do with fear, such as *frightened, scared, afraid, terrified, fearsome, terrible.*

◆ Examine the text for phrases and words that are particularly frightening or exciting. Ask the children to record their favourite examples with explanations of why they chose them.

◆ Ask the children to write a story that begins with a dream, a game or other similar device that ends at a crisis point when the lead character wakes up or ends the game.

◆ Find words in the text that the children are unsure of the meaning of, for example *quavering, unflinchingly, murk.* Encourage them to look them up in dictionaries or thesauruses and provide a glossary for other readers.

Genre
*contemporary
poem using
rhyming
couplets*

I Went Back

I went back after a cold
And nothing was the same.
When the register was called
Even my name
Sounded queer... new...
(And I was born here too!)
Everyone knew more than me,
Even Kenneth Hannaky
Who's worst usually.
They'd made a play
And puppets from clay
While I was away,
Learnt a song about Cape Horn,
Five guinea pigs were born.
Daffodils in the blue pot,
(I planted them)
Bloomed, and I was not
There to see.
Jean had a new coat
And someone, probably George,
Smashed my paper boat.
Monday was a dreadful day.
I wished I was still away.
Tuesday's news day.
I took my stamps to show,
Made a clown called Jo,
Learnt that song from John...
Cold's almost gone...
And... the smallest guinea pig,
Silky black and brown thing,
I'm having
Till spring.

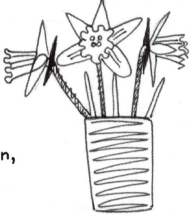

Gwen Dunn

I Went Back

Write up a list of how to make someone feel better when they've been ill, illustrated by the children. Provide some key vocabulary on the subject of illness and recovery.

PSHE and citizenship learning objectives

◆ To face new challenges (1c).
◆ To know about the range of jobs carried out by people who are trying to help them when they are sick or hurt (1e).
◆ To understand that there are different kinds of responsibilities, rights and duties at school and in the community (2d).
◆ To develop the skills to be effective in relationships, especially friendship (4c).

Background notes

This poem looks at an experience of a child going back to school after being ill and coping with the changes.

Vocabulary

Ill, sickness, isolated, behind.

Discussing the text

◆ Check that the children have understood what this poem is about. Who is speaking and what has happened to him or her? What is the setting? (The voice of the poem is a child who has been ill for a while and is coming back to school, finding that he or she has missed lots of things.)
◆ Ask the children if they have ever been ill and had to be off school for a week or more. What was it like? Refer the children to the vocabulary list you've made. If the children are struggling to remember, talk about your own experiences. (Perhaps feelings of misery; headaches; being listless, lonely, frustrated, sick, bored, tired; hurting.) This could be extended to talk about hospital stays and the problems facing children in that situation, where fear, possible pain and discomfort, lots of strangers and strange routines, and not always having a parent around to help them, are added to the experience.
◆ Ask the children to find parts of the poem that reveal the child's feelings, for example *Monday was a dreadful day. I wished I was still away.* Summarise the feelings on the board. Have the children ever felt like that?
◆ Do the class think the child was tempted to go home and ask if they could stay off some more? Would that help? (No. You have to get back into the swing. If the return were put off, it would be worse when the child did go back.) What happened as the week progressed? (The child started to get involved, to enjoy herself and feel better.) Ask the children what is good about coming back to school after being off ill? (For example, seeing friends, not being bored, feeling strong and well again.)
◆ How did John help the child to feel better about coming back? (He taught her the song they had learned whilst she was away.) Using examples from recent lessons, discuss with the children how they could help to make their friend or classmate feel better when they come back from being ill.

PSHE and citizenship activities

◆ Ask the children to write a story about a time when they have been ill. Prompt their thoughts with questions like *How did you feel when you were poorly? What happened when you came back to school? How did you feel?*

◆ Encourage the children to think about what images and words would cheer up a friend who is ill and design a card to send to him or her.

◆ In pairs, tell the children to list ways to help classmates and friends feel better when they come back from illness. Share the ideas with the whole class and together produce a word-processed guide to helping those who have been sick.

◆ Ask a children's nurse or play therapist from a local hospital to come and talk about having a stay in hospital. Perhaps arrange a visit to the local hospital. Alternatively, you might want to visit the hospital yourself and, with the nurse or play therapist, make a video to help dispel the children's fears.

◆ In small groups, ask the children to role-play a scene in which a child goes to visit a friend who is poorly. This could be at the friend's house or the hospital. Ask the children: *What would you take to your friend? What would you talk about? Would you play any games? What must you remember?* (That the friend is sick and you may need to go after a short while if he or she is tired or gets upset or cross.)

◆ Tell the children to find out in pairs about the professionals who help people when they are sick, for example doctors, nurses, physiotherapists, occupational therapists, speech therapists, radiographers and radiologists, pharmacists. Present the information in a booklet form for reference.

Further literacy ideas

◆ Look at the poem's use of rhyming couplets. Ask the children to copy six lines from the poem, match the rhyming words, then create another two lines that fit the context of the poem and rhyme.

◆ Help the children to rewrite the poem as a story, written in the third person, perhaps from John's point of view.

◆ In pairs, ask the children to discuss whether or not the poem's central character is a boy or a girl. Remind them to justify their reasoning when feeding back to the class.

◆ Ask the children to write a poem in verses, with the lead line for each verse *Coming back makes me feel…* Let them know that it doesn't have to rhyme. Alternatively, they could write a poem using the *Monday… Tuesday… Wednesday* format adopted in the second half of Gwen Dunn's poem.

Mike's Lonely Summer

Mike Myers is ten. He lives with his mum, dad and brother Jason.
One day, Mike's mum and dad have something to tell him…

Genre
contemporary fiction, with a non-fiction element, that discusses the issue of divorce

Mike came home from school one day, threw his books on the kitchen table, and headed for his room to change for football practice. But his Dad called to him from the living room. Mike thought it was strange that Dad was home early. Then he saw that the rest of the family sat waiting for him. Mum and Dad both looked so serious that Mike's stomach turned a somersault. Dad sat next to him and Mum held Jason on her lap.

"Boys, we have something important to tell you," Dad began. Then he swallowed hard and looked at Mum. But Mum only looked down at her hands in her lap, so Dad went on. "Your Mum and I have been fighting a lot for a long time. You've probably heard us shouting at each other. We always seem to make each other angry."

Mike remembered the time Mum had thrown a cup of hot coffee at Dad and the time Dad had been so angry that he shook the house when he slammed the back door. Then he screeched the car into the road.

Mum interrupted. "We love you, Mike, and we love you, Jason. You are our sons. But Dad and I don't love each other any more. And we get so angry when we're together that we've decided we should live apart. Your Father is moving to a flat tomorrow. We are getting a divorce."

Then Mum and Dad stopped and looked at Mike as if they expected him to say something. Mike wished they had stopped a lot sooner before they said that word *divorce*. A hundred questions came to his mind, but he couldn't think how to ask even one.

Carolyn Nystrom

- ◆ What is a divorce?
- ◆ Did I cause the divorce?
- ◆ Can I put things right?
- ◆ Who will look after me?
- ◆ Will I have to move?
- ◆ Who will have my birthday party?
- ◆ Is my Grandma still my Grandma if my Dad is gone?
- ◆ Why is God letting Mum and Dad divorce?
- ◆ Will Mum and Dad stop loving me, too?
- ◆ Can I still love both my Mum and Dad if they don't love each other?
- ◆ Will I have to take my Dad's place?
- ◆ If I pray, will God bring Mum and Dad back together?
- ◆ Who will make me be good?
- ◆ Can I phone my Dad if I need him?
- ◆ Will I always feel this bad?

Mike's Lonely Summer

Display a picture of Mike sitting alone. Alongside it, write up his feelings about the divorce and the questions he wants to ask.

PSHE and citizenship learning objectives

◆ To face new challenges positively (1c).
◆ To be aware of different types of relationship, including marriage and those between friends and families, and to develop skills to be effective in relationships (4c).
◆ To know where individuals and families can get help and support (4g).
◆ To recognise that divorce and separation are situations which they can do little to change.
◆ To recognise that they are not to blame for any unhappiness between their parents and that they are not responsible for making them happy.

Background notes

If there are any children in the class who are currently in the midst of parental separation or divorce, the use of this text might need to be postponed until they have had time to sufficiently recover their equilibrium. Be prepared in any event for disclosure and upset. Have some time set aside to talk to children on their own after the lesson or through the scheme.

Vocabulary

Divorce, separation, love, sadness.

Discussing the text

◆ Explain to the children that this story is fiction. Read the story, but not Mike's questions. Ask the children what is happening to Mike and Jason's family. Clarify the meaning of *divorce*. (When a married couple decide that they are going to end their marriage by a legal agreement and live apart.) Ask the children to put their hands up if they know of someone whose parents are divorced. (This is only to gauge the extent of their knowledge and understanding of the situation.) Confirm that most parents stay together and are happy with one another.

◆ Ask why Mike's parents are leaving one another and getting divorced, and list the children's responses on the board. (They don't love each other any more. They make one another angry.) Can the children think of any other reasons why parents might get a divorce? (For example, one of the partners has fallen in love with someone else, a problem like gambling, alcoholism or drug abuse may be making life difficult for the other partner and the children. Physical violence may be mentioned in the discussion. Accept it and endorse the point that no one should have to live with someone who is violent to them.)

◆ Read Mike's list of questions together and ask the children to help you find answers. Go through each question carefully and talk about the issues, first in the context of Mike's situation then, if appropriate, in other contexts. Issues that might arise from this discussion include the loss of friendship between parents and Mike having to live with that tension. The most important point is that it is not the child's fault or his responsibility to make things better. Practical problems like upheaval in moving and negotiating contact with each parent will be traumatic at first. Where possible, stress the positive outcomes – Mike will survive; things will get better; in the end, the parents are likely to be happier apart; both parents still love Mike.

PSHE and citizenship activities

◆ Explain to the children the importance of talking to someone at any time when they feel sad and troubled. If possible, this should be the children's parents but if that is difficult, or they don't seem to listen because they are so angry and upset, suggest that they could try talking to a grandparent, aunt, friend or even a friend's parents. The children could draw a spider diagram of people they can talk to about how they feel.

◆ Ask the children to pretend they are friends of Mike and he tells them what is happening. The children should write about what advice they would give him and how they could help him to feel a little better. Using these ideas, ask groups of children to create a friends' guide to helping when parents separate or divorce. Encourage a wide a series of responses, from *listening, sharing things and inviting them over* to *not pestering them about details*.

◆ Discuss the good things that can come from a divorce. For example, happier parents, sometimes two mums and two dads and more brothers and sisters, quality time with each parent, less worry if one of the parents has been difficult to get on with, less tension and bad-feeling at home, probably more presents.

Further literacy ideas

◆ Ask the children to write a conclusion to Mike's story. What happens to Mike and his family? Do they get back together or live apart more happily? How does Mike feel?

◆ Using five of the questions in the text, help the children to write a playscript conversation of questions and answers between Mike and his mum and dad.

◆ Look at Carolyn Nystrom's use of italic for the word *divorce*. Why did she do this and what does it add to the meaning of the text? Tell the children to word-process some sentences where they use italic or a different font to emphasise a particular word. How else can emphasis be made in words? (For example, inverted commas, capitals, font size, bold, different colours.)

◆ Ask the children look in the library for other texts that deal with the problem of divorce or separation. Explain that they can be non-fiction books, story books or poems. Each child should choose the one he or she thinks is best and write a review for the class.

Goodbye Max

Genre
contemporary poetic fiction that raises the issue of bereavement

Ben watched a red leaf fall to the ground.
It landed right near the place where Papa
had buried Max the week before.
"He was old," Papa said.
"I know," Ben answered. "But we were friends."
"A new dog can be a friend," Papa said.
Ben shook his head. "Not like Max."

When Papa brought home a puppy,
Ben didn't want to look at him.
"He's ugly," Ben said, "and he can't do anything."
"What should we call him?" Papa asked.
"Nothing," Ben said angrily. He went to his
room and slammed the door.

Zach came over to play ball,
but Ben wouldn't come down.
"Just for a little while," Zach shouted.
Ben shut the window.

Ben stretched out on his bed and put his
head under the pillow. It wasn't fair.

Holly Keller

Goodbye Max

Make a display entitled 'Helping Ben'. Draw Ben with his new puppy in his arms and add lines radiating out to brief descriptions of the ways Ben can be helped.

PSHE and citizenship learning objectives

◆ To know where individuals can get help and support (4g).

◆ To understand that when someone dies that we love, we feel very sad and gloomy for a while and that it is alright to have those feelings.

◆ To know how to be a good friend to someone who has lost a pet or a relative they cared about.

Background notes

This is a lovely story to help when children have lost a pet, to consider this type of loss and how to cope with those feelings. In its full form it shows how feelings change and how the kindness and patience of others helps Ben cope with his sadness and bereavement. It will work very well with Year 3 children and is a good introduction to bereavement from the death of a close relative or friend.

If a child has just lost a relative or very fond pet, it might be better to postpone this subject for several months or so to avoid any distress.

Vocabulary

Pet, death, care, love, sad, nasty, angry, funeral, bury.

Discussing the text

◆ Read the extract with the children. Ask who and what was Max. Confirm that Max was an old dog who was much loved by Ben and who became sick and died.

◆ Write Ben's name on a board or flip chart and ask the children to tell you how they think he is feeling. Write their suggestions around *Ben* on the board. Why is he feeling like this? (Because he loved Max and used to play with him and talk to him and do things with him. He misses him.)

◆ Do any of the children have a special pet that they love? Give children the chance to talk about these, firstly to a partner then to the class. Confirm that some pets can be very special to us.

◆ How do Ben's dad and Zach, his friend, try to help Ben feel better? (His dad talks to Ben, explaining why Max died and gets a new puppy. Zach asks him out to play.) What else could Ben's parents and friends do to help him? Refer to the display and list ideas on the board.

◆ How does Ben behave to his father and to his friend when he is so sad? (He is difficult and he is nasty about the puppy. He won't play with his friend.) Does this help Ben? Explain that it doesn't, but he might need to show how unhappy he is. Sometimes we do things that are silly or wrong when we are really upset. People who love and care for us will understand and forgive us.

◆ How do the children think Papa and the puppy felt after Ben stomped upstairs? What was wrong with Ben's behaviour here? (He was attacking others and hurting them because he was upset and hurt himself.)

◆ Ask the children if they have ever lost a pet. How did they feel? Who helped them to come to terms with it and in what ways?

PSHE and citizenship activities

◆ Ask the children to write about a special pet they have now or had in the past, or one they would like to have. Ask them: *Why is the pet so special? What do you do together?* Tell them to draw a picture of themselves with their pets to go with their text.

◆ The children could write a poem (possibly in free verse) in the first person, imagining themselves as Ben and describing his feelings about Max's death.

◆ Ask the children to imagine they are Zach and to write about what he does. How does he feel when Ben will not come down and play? What does he do then? Will he stop being Ben's friend or will he try again to help him?

◆ Help the children to role-play a scene in groups of three. Explain that one child is Ben, one is Ben's mum and one is Ben's dad. Advise the children to start the scene from Ben lying on his bed in misery, saying it wasn't fair. What do his mum and dad do and say? Ask each group to play the scene to the class, and then discuss the ways the parents try to help.

◆ Talk about the life cycle of animals. Explain that all living things have a natural life cycle. We all are born, grow, get old then die. Explain that when we care for and love our pets, it hurts when they die. We feel sad for a long while and that is OK. One of the ways we can mark the importance of this sadness is by burying the pet with a ceremony, like Ben's dad did in the garden. Ask children to plan a funeral service for Max, including the marking of Max's burial site (his grave). Why is this important? (So that Ben can visit the spot and think about Max.)

◆ Ask a funeral director to come in and talk to the children about formal pet funeral services and pet cemeteries, if there is one near by.

Further literacy ideas

◆ Ask the children to make a storyboard telling the last part of the story. What happens to Ben and the new puppy? Does Zach remain a friend?

◆ Look at the adjectives and adverb used in the text. List them in separate columns. Then ask the children for appropriate adverbs to add to these sentences from the extract:

"He was old," Papa said _____.

"I know," Ben answered _____.

"He's ugly," Ben said _____, "and he can't do anything."

He went to his room and slammed the door _____.

Together, list some new adjectives to describe how Ben is feeling as he lies on his bed.

◆ On the word processor, create and print an order of service for Max's funeral.

The Bombs Fall

This story is set in the Second World War. Harry is woken one night by an air raid. He and his parents and sister Dulcie go through the routine of going to the air raid shelter in the garden. They have done this many times before. Harry goes on ahead with the blankets and other important things and starts to prepare the air-raid shelter for the others.

Genre
historical
fiction

God, Mam and Dad were taking their time tonight. What was keeping them? That Jerry was getting closer. More guns were firing now. The garden, every detail of it, the bird-bath and the concrete rabbit, flashed black, white, black, white, black. There was a whispering in the air. Gun-shrapnel falling like rain… they shouldn't be out in *that*. Where were they? Where *were* they? Why weren't they tumbling through the shelter door, panting and laughing to be safe?

That Jerry was right overhead. *Vroomah. Vroomah. Vroomah.*

And then the other whistling. Rising to a scream. Bombs. Harry began to count. If you were still counting at ten, the bombs had missed you.

The last thing he remembered was saying "seven".

His back hurt and his neck hurt. His hands scrabbled, and scrabbled damp clay, that got under his fingernails. The smell told him he was still in the shelter, but lying on the damp floor. And a cautious, fearful voice, with a slight tremble in it, was calling out:

"Is anybody down there?"

Somebody pushed the curtain across the shelter door aside, and shone a torch on him. The person was wearing a warden's helmet, the white 'W' glimmering in the light of the torch. He thought at first it might be Dad. But it wasn't Dad. It had a big black moustache; it was a total stranger.

The stranger said, to somebody else behind him, "There's only one of them. A kid."

"Jesus Christ," said the somebody else. "Ask him where the rest are. There should be four in this shelter."

"Where's the rest, son? Where's your Mam and Dad?"

"In the… I don't know."

"D'you mean, still in the house, son?"

The voice behind muttered. "Christ, I hate this job." Then it said, with a sharp squeak of fear, "What's that?"

"What's *what*?"

"Something soft under me foot. Shine your light."

"'S only a rabbit. A dead rabbit."

"Thank God. Hey, son, can you hear me? Can you get up? Are you hurt?"

Why didn't the man come down and help him? What was he so *frightened* of?

Harry got up slowly. He hurt nearly all over, but not so badly that he couldn't move. The man gave him a hand and pulled him up out of the shelter. Harry peered up the garden. He could see quite well because the sky to the west was glowing pink.

There was no greenhouse left.

There was no house left. The houses to each side were still standing, though their windows had gone, and their slates were off.

"Where's our house?"

There was a silence. Then the man with the moustache said, "What's yer name, son?" Harry told him.

"And what was yer Dad's name? And yer Mam's?" He wrote it all down in a notebook, like the police did, when thy caught you scrumping apples. He gave them Dulcie's name, too. He tried to be helpful. Then he said, "Where *are* they?" and began to run up the garden path.

The man grabbed him, quick and rough.

"You can't go up there, son. There's a gas leak. A bad gas leak. Pipe's fractured. It's dangerous. It's against the law to go up there…"

"But my Mum and Dad're up there…"

"Nobody up there now, son. Come down to the Rest Centre. They'll tell you all about it at the Rest Centre."

Harry just let himself be led off across some more gardens. It was easy, because all the fences were blown flat. They went up the path of Number Five. The white faces of the Humphreys, who lived at Number Five, peered palely from the door of their shelter. They let him pass, without saying anything to him.

In the road, the wardens who

were leading him met two other wardens.

"Any luck at Number Nine?"

"Just this lad…"

There was a long, long silence. Then one of the other wardens said, "We found the family from Number Seven. They were in the garden. The bomb caught them as they were running for the shelter…"

"They all right?"

"Broken arms and legs, I think. But they'll live. Got them away in the ambulance."

Harry frowned. The Simpsons lived at Number Seven. There was some fact he should be able to remember about the Simpsons. But he couldn't. It was all… mixed up.

"Come on, son. Rest Centre for you. Can you walk that far?"

Harry walked. He felt like screaming at them. Only that wouldn't be a very British thing to do. But something kept building up inside him; like the pressure in his model steam-engine.

Where *was* his steam-engine?

Where was Mam, who could cuddle him and make everything all right?

Where was Dad in his warden's uniform, who would sort everything out?

Next second he had broken from their hands, and was running up another garden path like a terrified rabbit. He went through another gate, over the top of

another air-raid shelter, through a hedge that scratched him horribly. on, and on, and on.

He heard voices calling him as he crouched in hiding. They seemed to call a long time. Then one of them said, "That wasn't very clever."

"It's shock. Shock takes them funny ways. You can never tell how shock's going to take them."

"Hope he's not seriously hurt, poor little bleeder."

"Kid that can run like that…?"

And then their voices went away, leaving him alone.

Robert Westall

The Bombs Fall

Display a scene from the story, perhaps of a bombed house, an Anderson shelter and Harry emerging out of it into the care of the air-raid wardens.

PSHE and citizenship learning objectives

◆ To discuss topical issues and problems (2a).

◆ To think about the lives and experiences of people during the Second World War in Britain (4b).

◆ To understand that their feelings affect themselves and others, to care about other people's feelings and try to see things from their points of view. (4c).

◆ To know where individuals can get help and support (4g).

◆ To understand that when someone dies that we love, we feel shocked and miserable for a long while and that those feelings are normal.

◆ To know how to be a good friend to someone who has lost a relative they loved.

Background notes

This text works best with Year 5 or 6 classes and naturally fits into study of World War II as part of the curriculum history theme 'Britain since 1930'. The historical setting can help children to cope with the idea of bereavement and loss at a psychological distance, however, if any child has been bereaved of a close relative within the year, it would be better to postpone use of this text.

The extract includes some bad language and blasphemy. You may feel it appropriate to delete this or mention it as possibly being offensive.

Vocabulary

Shock, air raid, bomb, shelter, warden, death, trauma.

Discussing the text

◆ Read the first part of the text, to the point when the bomb fell as Harry had counted to seven. Make sure the children are aware of what is happening. Ask them what the purpose of the shelter is. What does Harry mean when he says *That Jerry was getting closer*? (Jerry is a slang name for the Germans.) What are Harry's feelings during this passage and how do they change?

◆ Read the rest of the extract. What has happened? Who are the men in the garden and what are they doing? (They are air-raid wardens whose job was to account for the losses during the bombing and get people to safety.) How do we know that? (The questions they ask, the white *W* on the helmet.) One of the men says *I hate this job!* Why do the children think he says that?

◆ What did Harry see when he first came out of the shelter? What was his reaction? At what point does Harry become aware of what has happened? (When he ran up the garden path to search for his family.) Why did the men stop him? (It was dangerous. They wouldn't have wanted Harry to see his dead parents.) Obliquely, the men tell Harry that his parents are dead. Ask the children to find the sentences that tell us this. Why were the men not direct, telling him his parents had been killed in the bomb blast?

◆ What happens on the way to the rest centre? What is Harry trying to do? (Find his family.) The men say Harry is in a state of shock. What does that mean? (He is unable to act or talk sensibly. He can't take in what is happening to him and what has happened to his family. He needs time to rest and someone to talk to.) Is there anything in the text that confirms this state of shock? (He cannot accept his parents' death. He runs away from help, he wanted to scream, he felt pressure building up inside him.)

◆ How realistic is Robert Westall's account? Would many children be in Harry's position?

◆ Could Harry's parents be alive? If so, how? (Develop a range of possible ideas.) Ask the children what they think will happen next. Will his parents be found alive? If not, will Harry survive without them? What will happen to him?

PSHE and citizenship activities

◆ Discuss with the whole class the ways someone copes when they suffer a sudden trauma or loss like this. What do they need? What should Harry have done? (Sought help from relatives or the Rest Centre.) If Harry has relatives what are they likely to do when they hear what has happened?

◆ In small groups, the children could role-play a scene when Harry's relatives come to search for him. Encourage the children to think about how Harry feels when he is found and how his relatives feel. As a class, watch all the performances, looking for common ideas in the scenes, then summarise the feelings of those involved.

◆ As a class, make a spider diagram showing Harry's feelings about the death of his parents. Brainstorm as many words as possible to describe these feelings.

◆ How will Harry feel about the Germans now? Will those feelings stay with him as he grows up or will they change when the war ends? Ask the children to discuss this in small groups and be ready to feed back to the whole class. What is unhealthy about holding on to grievances? Do they think German children hated British pilots for killing their parents?

◆ Invite someone in to talk about what it was like to be a child during the war. Include discussion of how they coped during the Blitz and, if appropriate, what they feel about the Germans nowadays.

◆ Discuss the problems facing a child today who has lost their family in, for example, a car accident. Who would help them and what would happen to them? Stress that this is rare and focus on the positive here – there will be lots of help from family and friends and the social and medical services. You could introduce the subject of foster care or adoption, but care is needed if you have children in this position in the class. Ask: *If someone in our class were to suffer this way, how can we help, both at the time it happens and when they come back to school?* Let the children discuss this in pairs and work out a list of ways to help *either* at the time of the death or when the child returns. Share everyone's ideas.

Further literacy ideas

◆ In pairs, get the to children talk about what Harry would need to survive in the long run, if he has no relatives and refuses to go for help to the Rest Centre. Ask them to write a list and a plan of action for him.

◆ Look at the author's use of dialogue to transmit ideas and the plot. The children could write a discussion between the two air-raid wardens after they have left Harry, conveying some idea of what will happen to Harry next. Remind the children to use speech marks and punctuation correctly.

◆ See if the children can write a poem from Harry's point of view, describing what happened to him that night and how he felt. Tell them to focus on using the most effective words from the spider diagram (see PSHE and citizenship activities).

◆ Ask the children to examine the text for words that are in dialect or slang, listing them with standard English versions alongside. For example *Jerry* – Germans, *yer* – your, *Mam* – Mum.

◆ Ask the children to work out, in note form, two contrasting plot developments for the story. They should choose which one they prefer and justify that choice.

CHAPTER 5 Managing conflict

The process of teaching children to resist the instinct to fight to get their own way or to release their own wrath through violence is one undertaken daily in the playground and sometimes in the classroom. Occasionally, the advice from parents is to 'hit back twice as hard if hit', and this doesn't aid the task.

Conflict in our lives is normal, whether it is because of a disagreement, a misunderstanding, clash of personality or a direct provocation by someone deliberately intending to achieve our submission. Learning to manage conflict helps us to maintain our own self-respect yet inflict no, or minimal, harm on others.

Conflict in school usually results from threats, perceived or real, to territory or property (*It's my ball/pencil/book!*, *This is my chair/desk/hook/place in the queue!*), challenges to perceived rights (*It's my turn, I go first, I chose who plays, She's my friend!*) or as a reaction to hurt, usually caused by joking or teasing or deliberate taunting (*I'm not a coward, I'll get you for that!*).

The instinct to protect rights, possessions and territory, to defend self-esteem and retaliate, means that learning the skills of assertiveness, communication and compromise is difficult. However, it is worth working with children on these skills to reduce the trouble in the playground and classroom, to make the lives of children more enjoyable and to support these children when they grow up and find that the penalties for fighting can be grave.

Bullying is also covered in this chapter in some depth. The desire to bully is ever present in a few children. Its causes vary. Low self-esteem is sometimes the cause, or bullying behaviour can be learned at home as a normal part of the strategies used to get your own way and what you want. Some children bully because they were bullied when they were smaller. Others act this way because they enjoy the power buzz it gives them. Whatever the cause, it is wrong. Bullying can be defined in many different ways but it is generally assumed to be a deliberate act to hurt or frighten someone of less power than oneself, for pleasure or gain.

These texts try to examine the causes of bullying, expound upon the strategies for preventing and dealing with bullying and challenge, through Jan Needle's work *The Bully*, the stereotyping of bullies. Each set of text activities, whilst focusing on a particular aspect of bullying, also includes work on strategies to get help if being bullied. This aspect is important to include whenever bullying appears on the curriculum to reinforce the availability of help to the victim. Each of the texts is suitable for a different age group. Caution will need to be employed if there are children currently known, or expected to be, victims of bullying.

This chapter also examines the differing types of conflict – the squabble amongst friends and the more harmful betrayal by friends. The final text is part of the process for mediation, that technique needed for bystanders and friends to enable them to become peacemakers rather than partisan supporters, or helpless watchers, as two people hurt each other by words and actions.

The principles of the behaviour policy and mission statement of the school can be incorporated into this work to provide a powerful link to the local environment.

Being a bully is not all fun

Genre
information
(humorous)

It is not all fun being a bully.
It is NOT fun for *them*…

Nobody likes you…
Not even most of your gang. They are just scared of you.

If you are found out they won't stick up for you. Everybody likes to bully a bully!

You may not like yourself.
Maybe you would prefer to have friends, to be looked up to.
Nobody wants to be your friend.

Some people are even sorry for you…

Child's Play (International) Ltd

Being a bully is not all fun

Display a picture of a male and female bully, with questions surrounding them as they have doubts about their bullying.

PSHE and citizenship learning objectives

◆ To research, discuss, and debate topical issues, problems and events (2a).

◆ To realise the consequences of anti-social and aggressive behaviours, such as bullying on individuals and communities (2c).

◆ To know the school rules about where to get help (3g).

◆ To realise the nature and consequences of racism, teasing, bullying and aggressive behaviours and how to respond to them and ask for help (4d).

◆ To recognise and challenge stereotypes of bullies and victims (4e).

Background notes

This extract is from *Bully For You* (produced by Child's Play International), an excellent resource book for all Key Stage 2 children that deals with aspects of bullying in a stark and hard-hitting way, with dark humour and powerful points.

Vocabulary

Bullying, bully, gang, friends, victim, take turns.

Discussing the text

◆ Before you read the text, ask the children what they think bullying is. Record their ideas on a flip chart, then summarise them. Try to get the children to understand that bullying is any deliberate act to hurt or frighten someone for pleasure or gain.

◆ Ask the children what the difference is between squabbling and bullying. (One is two people of more or less equal power arguing with one another. The other is unprovoked and perpetrated by a stronger person onto someone less powerful.)

◆ How can the children recognise a bully? This should produce some interesting stereotypes that might need challenging, but focus on the behaviours and social grouping that often come with bullying activity, for example gangs or groups, picking on people, taunting and teasing, pushing them around, forcing them to do things, threatening them.

◆ Ask the children why they think bullies bully. Write down the children's suggestions, then re-read the text. Confirm the children's understanding that, whatever bullies may think is good or fun about what they do, they are in fact hurting themselves as well as others.

◆ Who is the text referring to when it says *It is NOT fun for them*? (Those who are being bullied, those who have to see others being bullied, the teachers who have to deal with bullying, parents whose children bully or are bullied.) On the flip chart, write the word *bullying*, and radiate from that all the people who are hurt or upset by the bullying.

◆ Ask: *Is it true that nobody likes you if you are a bully? Why?* (Because you rule friends with fear. You can turn on your friends and bully them and they resent that, they often think it's not fun to hurt others, it makes your gang feel uncomfortable and in the wrong, you and they get into trouble too easily, you can't find good games to play.)

◆ *Would bullies prefer to have real friends rather than a gang? Perhaps they don't know how to be a friend. How can we help bullies to stop bullying and become friends?* (Making sure they know you won't accept bullying if they are your friends, teaching them to share and take turns, stopping them if they start being nasty and getting them to enjoy other games and activities.)

◆ The text concludes with the sentence *Some people are even sorry for you…* Do the children agree with that? Will these people do well in life and enjoy themselves, or will they get into trouble and find themselves lonely and unloved and unhappy? Children are likely to find this view difficult to accept, but try to reduce the potency of the 'all-powerful bully' by introducing the idea of a sad person who doesn't know how to behave well yet.

PSHE and citizenship activities

◆ Ask the children to write a story from the point of view of a bully in which the bully is befriended and shown how to stop bullying.

◆ Help the children to role-play a scene where a bully is caught. In small groups, tell them to act out the scene with one person playing the bully, one the headteacher, and two the parents of the bully. Ask the groups to perform their scenes to the class.

◆ The children could write a poem describing the feelings of someone who is being bullied.

◆ In small groups, ask the children to work out a series of ways a person who is being bullied can get help. (For example, tell a teacher, a friend or a parent; say *No* loudly to anything the bully demands and stand up to the bully; stick together with your friends.)

◆ In pairs, ask the children to convert the text into a brief guide about bullies, to use and share with other classes, including, for example, *Bullies do not always have fun. Bullies are not liked by anybody. Bullies get caught and get into trouble.*

◆ Using the work done so far, prepare a class assembly on the problem of bullying to explain what bullying is, how people feel when they are bullied, how to get help and what happens when the bully gets caught. Bring it to a close by saying that the bully is behaving badly, but is also probably quite lonely and angry. He or she needs help to learn to behave better and have more fun and friends.

Further literacy ideas

◆ Look closely at the text. What sort of text is it? (Information.) Who is it directed at? (It is addressed to the bully.) How do you know that? (The use of the word *you*.) Ask the children to rewrite a portion of the text, translating it into the third person.

◆ Tell the children to look at the way the text uses ellipses (…). *What do they mean? Why are they being used in this text?* (It means there is more that could be said but that has been left out.) The children could take one of the sentences each and complete the sentence with text of their own.

◆ Examine the text for whole words made up of capital letters, and the use of exclamation marks and italics. What is the purpose of these? (To emphasise the words.) Ask the children to write some sentences, using these devices to stress important or powerful words or meanings.

Are there ways to stop bullying?

*Genre
information
diagram*

Trying to understand your own feelings can help you to

judge when it is best to leave a situation

share what is happening with others

see you don't have to be liked by everyone

look confident even when you are afraid

DIGITAL STOCK

recognise how others are feeling

and get on with others.

tell others how you feel without being afraid

stop going along with things you really don't want to do

judge when and how to stand up for yourself and others

Angela Grunsell

Are there ways to stop bullying?

Display a summary of the information from discussions, presented in a similar way with examples and illustrations of the strategies.

PSHE and citizenship learning objectives

◆ To face new challenges positively by collecting information, looking for help, making responsible decisions and taking action to combat bullying (1c).

◆ To research, discuss, and debate topical issues, problems and events (2a).

◆ To realise the consequences of anti-social and aggressive behaviours, such as bullying, on individuals and communities (2c).

◆ To recognise that pressure to behave in an unacceptable way can come from people they know and how to ask for help and use basic techniques for resisting pressure to do wrong (3f).

◆ To know the school rules about where to get help (3g).

◆ To realise the nature and consequences of racism, teasing, bullying and aggressive behaviours and how to respond to them and ask for help (4d).

Background notes

This text works very well with children from Years 4 and 5.

Vocabulary

Bullying, teasing, strategies, bully, victim, bystander, stand up, frightened, threatened, intimidated, coward, respect, confident.

Discussing the text

◆ What is this text telling us? Discuss with the children what bullying behaviour is and why it is wrong. Stress that we all have a right to be respected and to be allowed to live without being deliberately frightened, threatened and hurt by someone else.

◆ Look at the diagram together. Explain that the phrases on the left-hand side refer to children who are being made to join in with the bullying or do stupid and dangerous things by a bully who is a leader. The right-hand side contains advice to a victim who is being frightened or threatened by a bully. Read the text together, first the left-hand, then the right side. The diagram includes two key phrases at the top and bottom, designed to introduce and conclude the advice.

◆ Start at the top left box and discuss the advice given here. What does *judge when it is best to leave a situation* mean? What are the risks in not getting involved? (The bully gets nastier or makes others shun that person. He or she might be called a coward.) Ask: *What could happen if you stay in the situation?* Look at the second box and explain that sometimes we have to put up with others not liking us because we won't join in with doing nasty or silly things. The third box advises us to *recognise how others are feeling*. Explain that if someone is being hurt by his or her friend, the children need to realise how that feels, by imagining themselves in the same situation. Suggest that they try to stop the hurt by telling the friend to stop. What are the problems with this? (The friend turns on them and hurts them instead.) Do we do nothing then? (No, we get help from an adult.) Finally, the box at the bottom advises the children not to go along with things they don't want to be involved in. Talk about the pressure to do what friends are doing even though you know it is wrong. How do we feel when we are doing things we don't want to? (Frightened of getting into trouble, we don't enjoy ourselves, we get angry or frustrated and feel bad about what we're doing.) What is at stake?

◆ Discuss the other side of the diagram. Start with *share what is happening with others. Who could we share our feelings and fears with?* What advice would the children give to someone who was being bullied and was frightened of what the bully might do to them? Why does the box say *look confident even when you are afraid*? (Bullies tend to avoid the confident.) Stress to the children that if they are being bullied, they shouldn't be frightened to tell someone. The bully relies on their victims not telling anyone. The only way to stop a bully is to get help from adults. The final box of advice suggests that sometimes it is worth standing up to a bully, refusing to do as he or she says and ignoring the threats. Bullies take it for granted that their victims are intimidated. They want to avoid real trouble and they can be cowards. Tell the children not to fight them, but refuse to be frightened and upset. Advise them to report the bully to a teacher or other adult if the trouble continues.

P SHE and citizenship activities

◆ In small groups, ask the children to use a large piece of paper to write some good advice to a friend who is being bullied, a friend who is bullying or a bystander who has watched someone being bullied. Let each group present their advice to the rest of the class, then make word-processed copies for display.

◆ As a whole class, design a questionnaire to find out if children from other classes have been bullied or have seen people being bullied. Discuss the particular problems that a survey on bullying might raise and how the issues can be addressed. For example, some children may be afraid to report that they are being bullied and one solution may be to allow children to complete the survey anonymously. Younger children may confuse bullying with disputes and fighting and it may therefore be a good idea to explain to each class what bullying behaviour is before giving them the questionnaire. Children can take responsibility for conducting the survey, then analysing the results and presenting them to the school in an assembly. Include the children's advice on how to combat bullying in that assembly too.

◆ As a class, discuss ways of preventing bullying happening in the first place. (The children could brainstorm ideas around issues of supervision, zero tolerance, having a clear attitude that being nasty is wrong, being a good friend, being warm and welcoming to newcomers and those who seem lonely, not teasing anyone.) Any ideas for implementation could be presented to the headteacher or the school council.

◆ Bring in someone from Kidscape or a similar team to work with the class and school on preventing and tackling bullying.

Further literacy ideas

◆ Look at the format of the diagram and ask the children to recreate in pairs their own information diagram, using the advice from the group discussion. Help them to use the word processor to create the boxes and arrows.

◆ Look at different forms of information diagrams in other books. Which designs do the children find work best and why?

◆ Ask the children to write a play in pairs, that includes a conversation between a bully and a victim who is standing up for him or herself.

◆ Ask the children to think of as many words as they can that describe the feelings of a victim and those of a bully, then write a poem using the best of these words, from the point of view either of a bully or a victim.

The Bully

Simon Mason is a simple lump of a boy who has a reputation for getting into and causing trouble and for lying. He comes from the rough end of town. But is he a bully? What is certain is that he's being got at. Today he decides that attack is the best form of defence. Getting ready for the inevitable taunting and violence he arms himself with a stone. Unfortunately, a teacher sees.

Genre
contemporary
fiction by an
established
writer

Anna Royle was a tall girl for her age. Tall, and confident and very nice. Rebekkah Tanner was her best friend and her neighbour, and their two houses were rather isolated from everybody else's. Because of this, perhaps, they were very close.

They had talked about the Simon Mason problem as they were driven into school by Anna's mother, and Anna and Rebekkah had discussed it on the phone quite late the night before. David, who had gone to bed earlier than his sister, being younger, wanted to know what they had decided. As usual, he had opened his mouth too wide and put his foot in it.

"What was that, David?" asked their mother, from the front. "Did you say bullying?"

Anna glared at him. Even the back of the Volvo estate was not vast enough for them to talk in private.

"Not exactly bullying, Mrs Royle," put in Rebekkah politely. "It's just the games this morning. Sometimes some of the boys get rough, that's all."

"It's more enthusiasm than anything," added Anna, smiling at her friend. "You know how David exaggerates, the little squirt."

Mrs Royle glanced backwards. She had a strong face like her daughter's, although not quite so attractive.

"Don't you listen to them, David, you're not a little squirt at all." She paused. "You would tell me, though, wouldn't you? If there was really any nastiness like that?"

The children made faces at each other. She was worrying about the school again. *Her* mother, their gran, had always disapproved about them going to a State school. They were the first ones in the family who ever had.

"Oh, Mum," said Anna. "Don't start that again. It's a *good* school, St Michael's, we have a great time there."

"And anyway," said Rebekkah, "we've got David, haven't we? He's a match for *any* rough boy!"

The woman and the girls joined in the laughter, while David stared stolidly through the window at the crowds of children heading for the gate. Sometimes he felt ganged up on.

"Ah well," said Mrs Royle, as the doors were opened and they piled on to the pavement. "I suppose you're right. There seem so *many* of them, though. Are you *quite* sure that…"

But the children, and Rebekkah, were hurtling round the throng, school-bags and games kit flying out behind them.

Certainly, she told herself, they seemed happy enough. She put the Volvo into gear and nosed it gently through the crowds of milling children.

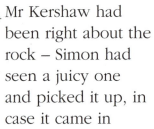

Some of them looked so very *rough*, she thought.

Mr Kershaw had been right about the rock – Simon had seen a juicy one and picked it up, in case it came in useful for the ambush. He had seen the Volvo pull up by the kerb and had ducked behind the old pavilion with a sudden mix of fear and excitement in his stomach. He had the rock, he had the keyring. Maybe they hadn't seen him, though.

They had, and retribution was extremely swift. Simon had tripped over his foot in getting to the place, dropped his towel, scattering the kit. He was on one knee when Anna burst around the corner.

"He's armed!" she shouted, jubilantly. "The little spassie's armed!"

Simon's fantasies of warfare and revenge lay in the mud, scattered like his dirty football gear. He got clumsily to his feet as David joined Anna, his stomach going hollow. Rebekkah's tousled head appeared, then she took station at the corner to keep a watch-out.

"Simon, Simon, little Simple Simon!" chanted David. "Spastic, spastic, spastic!"

Simon let the hand that held the rock drop to his side. To Anna it was obvious what he was hoping for.

"You can't fool me!" she shouted. "I can see the stone! You were going to throw it at me, weren't you? You're a bully, aren't you?"

As she darted in to hit him she was laughing. Simon's face – rather round and hopeless – twisted in his fear. But he was trying, also, to form a smile. A supplicating smile, a pleading smile, ingratiating.

"Yerk!" went Anna Royle, in mock disgust. "You're a creep as well!"

She danced up to him and punched him in the face, feeling his nose bend squashily beneath her knuckles. As she drew her hand away, his face crumpled satisfyingly. There would be tears.

"Look out!" Rebekkah hissed. "Miss is coming! Miss Shaw!"

She sounded frightened. She'd left it too late, she'd forgotten to look out because she'd wanted to watch the fun.

"Simple Simon!" chanted David, and Rebekkah squeaked to interrupt him.

"Shut *up*! Shut *up*!" It was a cross between a whisper and a cry. Two seconds later Louise Shaw strode purposefully into sight. But not before Anna had dropped her school bag and her rolled towel to the ground and spread it with a kick. Not before she had dropped to one knee and put a look of anguish on her face.

"Oh, Miss," she cried, "he hit me, Miss, he hit me!"

To the children, it was just a game…

Jan Needle

The Bully

Make a display on bullying around an image of Simon Mason, itemising the reasons why bullying is wrong on one side and the means of combating bullying on the other.

PSHE and citizenship learning objectives

◆ To realise the consequences of anti-social and aggressive behaviours, such as bullying, on individuals and communities (2c).

◆ To know that there are different kinds of responsibilities, rights and duties at home, and that these can sometimes conflict (2d).

◆ To recognise that pressure to behave in an unacceptable way can come from people they know and how to ask for help and use basic techniques for resisting pressure to do wrong (3f).

◆ To know the school rules about where to get help (3g).

◆ To realise the nature and consequences of racism, teasing, bullying and aggressive behaviours and how to respond to them and ask for help (4d).

◆ To recognise and challenge stereotypes of bullies and victims (4e).

Background notes

This story challenges the expected ideas of who bullies are, for example male, large and stupid. It works best with Year 6 children as they can best appreciate the subtlety of the situation.

Vocabulary

Bully, victim, retaliation, injustice, violence, taunt, gang.

Discussing the text

◆ Read the text and confirm with the children the gist of the story. (Simon is determined to hurt Anna. Anna, her brother David and friend Rebekkah are a gang. They taunt Simon. Anna punches Simon in an organised attack. When the teacher comes Anna fakes an attack on herself.)

◆ Who is the bully? Allow children to discuss this in pairs, then ask for feedback. List the evidence for Anna and Simon, using deductions and reference to the text. Add David and Rebekkah to the list. Are they bullies? (They are the bullies here because they *actively* take part in the act of bullying and they show no anxiety or doubt. Simon's situation is less clear, but on this occasion he is a victim following aggressive behaviour.) Allow the children some ambiguity of feeling and encourage them to judge by the degree of deliberate, unprovoked harm intended.

◆ Who seems to be *nice* and is from a well-off family worried about *rough* children? (Anna.) Would the children normally expect someone like her to be a bully? Why do they think she is being violent and cruel and enjoying it?

◆ Ask the children: *What is so wrong about bullying?* (It's cruel, can make people deeply miserable, and is unfair.)

◆ How will the teacher react to this scene? What will go against Simon in the first instance? (His reputation as a troublemaker and liar. Anna probably seems like a good girl to teachers and parents.)

◆ Ask the children what they should do if they see or hear of anyone being bullied. (Report it, even if it is a suspicion, watch closely to catch the children in the act, intervene if possible, at least verbally, and help the victim to report it by supporting them.)

◆ *What are the problems in trying to stop bullying?* (You can become a target yourself.) *How do you overcome that?* (Through collective support and protection of friends, immediate reporting of any threats or intimidation, avoid being sucked into conflict, tell a parent if you can't tell a teacher.)

◆ *What do you do if your friend is the bully?* This needs considerable discussion as it raises issues of conflict of loyalty and duty. (Ultimately, you will have to sacrifice the friendship rather than collude with a cruel act. Advise the bully to stop, even if you are turned upon.) *In the end, should you be friends with someone who wants to pick on and hurt others?*

◆ Discuss what might happen next in the story. Allow for a range of responses, but talk about the risk of injustice and the problems of getting a bad reputation.

◆ The extract ends with the line *To the children, it was just a game… Was it? Is it ever?*

PSHE and citizenship activities

◆ Ask the children to write the next chapter of the story. What happens to Simon? How does he defend himself or does he remain silent? Will Anna and her gang get away with it?

◆ The children could write a poem from the point of view of Simon as he faces the teacher. How does he feel? He is not an angel and can be violent. Make sure the poem reflects the subtleties of this situation and his character.

◆ Look at stereotypes as a whole class. Ask the children to describe a typical bully (for example, big, strong, tough-looking, nasty, stupid, male) and a typical victim (perhaps small, weak, 'different', female or male). Compare the characters in the story to these images. How do they fit in? How 'true' are the stereotypes? Give some examples from real life of people who have been victims of bullying, including some who later went on to be successful and famous, such as the swimmer Duncan Goodhew who

was bullied as a child. (Kidscape may be able to provide you with more information and further examples.) Ask the children in pairs to create and word-process a play about bullying, in which stereotypes are challenged.

◆ Help the children to role-play the end scene from the text. In small groups, tell them to work out the next scene in one of two ways – either when Simon receives justice or the reverse, when Anna wins. Share the scenes, then discuss the ways forward for Simon, and what Anna and her gang will do in either situation. Stress the positive, and that we shouldn't have to accept injustice or perpetual violence and cruelty.

◆ In groups, ask the children to draft some advice for younger children who are being bullied. These can then be presented to younger classes.

Further literacy ideas

◆ Identify words in the text that are used to hurt people. Ask the children to add others from experience and write an explanation about why each of these words hurt. Consider the maxim *Sticks and stones can hurt my bones but words can never harm me.* Is it true? The children should then create a positive rule about the words spoken to other people.

◆ How does Jan Needle vividly create the characters of Simon and Anna? (By using adjectives, realistic dialogue and adverbs associated with that dialogue.) Under the subheadings *Anna* and *Simon*, tell the children to record the key words and phrases from the text that create images in our minds of these two people.

The Sword in the Stone

PHOTOCOPIABLE

Genre
classical
historical
novel
(humorous
fantasy)

This story is about the young King Arthur as a boy, learning about life from his magical tutor Merlyn. It is set in medieval times when knights held jousts or tournaments to fight against one another in competition.
The extract begins in the woods where two elderly knights in armour, King Pellinore and Sir Grummore, have met to joust. From the safety of the trees, Wart (young King Arthur) and Merlyn watch. Both knights have become unseated and are now fighting on foot, wielding heavy swords. Sir Grunmore has the upper hand and asks the king if he wants to make peace.

"Pax," said King Pellinore, mumbling rather.

Then, just as Sir Grummore was relaxing with the fruits of victory, he swung round upon him, shouted "Non!" at the top of his voice, and gave him a good push in the middle of the chest.

Sir Grummore fell over backwards.

"Well!" exclaimed the Wart. "What a cheat! I would not have thought it of him."

King Pellinore hurriedly sat on his victim's chest, thus increasing the weight upon him to a quarter of a ton and making it quite impossible for him to move, and began to undo Sir Grummore's helm.

"You said Pax!"

"I said Pax Non under my breath."

"It's a swindle."

"It's not."

"You're a cad."

"No, I'm not."

"Yes, you are."

"I said Pax Non."

"You said Pax."

"No, I didn't."

"Yes, you did."

"No, I didn't."

"Yes, you did."

By this time Sir Grummore's helm was unlaced and they could see his bare head glaring at King Pellinore, quite purple in the face.

"Yield thee, recreant," said the King.

"Shan't," said Sir Grummore.

"You know you have to yield, or I shall cut off your head."

"Cut it off then."

"Oh, come on," said the King. "You know you have to yield when your helm is off."

"Feign I," said Sir Grummore.

"Well, I shall just cut your head off."

"I don't care."

The King waved his sword menacingly in the air.

"Go on," said Sir Grummore. "I dare you to."

The King lowered his sword and said, "Oh, I say, do yield, please."

"You yield," said Sir Grummore.

"But I can't yield. I am on top of you after all, am I not, what?"

"Well, I have feigned yieldin'."

"Oh, come on, Grummore. I do think you are a cad not to yield. You know very well I can't cut your head off."

"I would not yield to a cheat who started fightin' after he said Pax."

"I am not a cheat."

"You are a cheat."

"No, I'm not."

"Yes, you are."

"No, I'm not."

"Yes, you are."

"Very well," said King Pellinore. "You can jolly well get up and put on your helm and we will have a fight. I won't be called a cheat for anybody."

"Cheat!" said Sir Grummore.

They stood up and fumbled together with the helm, hissing, "No, I'm not" – "Yes, you are," until it was safely on. Then they retreated to opposite ends of the clearing, got their weight upon their toes, and came rumbling and thundering together like two runaway trams.

Unfortunately they were now so cross that they had both ceased to be vigilant, and in the fury of the moment they missed each other altogether. The momentum of their armour was too great for them to stop till they had passed each other handsomely, and then they manoeuvred about in such a manner that neither happened to come within the other's range of vision. It was funny watching them, because King Pellinore, having already been caught from behind once, was continually spinning round to look behind him, and Sir Grummore, having used the stratagem himself, was doing the same thing. Thus they wandered for some five minutes, standing still, listening, clanking, crouching, creeping, peering, walking on tiptoe, and occasionally making a chance swipe behind their backs. Once they were standing within a few feet of each other, back to back, only to stalk off in opposite directions with infinite precaution, and once King Pellinore did hit Sir Grummore with one of his back strokes, but they both immediately spun round so often that they became giddy and mislaid each other afresh.

After five minutes Sir Grummore said, "All right, Pellinore. It is no use hidin'. I can see where you are."

"I am not hiding," exclaimed

King Pellinore indignantly. "Where am I?"

They discovered each other and went up close together, face to face.

"Cad," said Sir Grummore.

"Yah," said King Pellinore.

They turned round and marched off to their corners, seething with indignation.

"Swindler," shouted King Pellinore.

"Beastly bully," shouted King Pellinore.

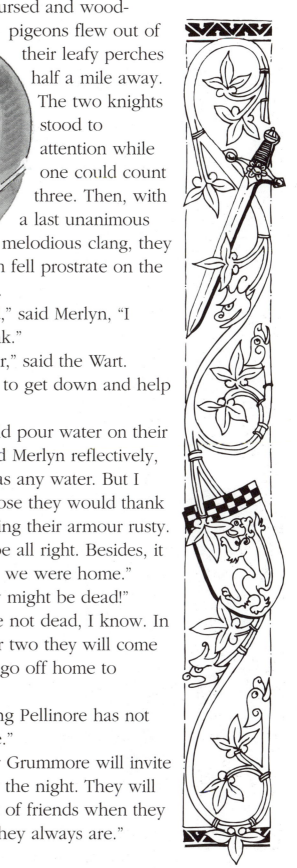

With this they summoned all their energies together for one decisive encounter, leaned forward, lowered their heads like two billy-goats, and positively sprinted together for the final blow. Alas, their aim was poor. They missed each other by about five yards, passed at full steam doing at least eight knots, like ships that pass in the night but speak not to each other in passing, and hurtled onwards to their doom. Both knights began waving their arms like windmills, anti-clockwise, in the vain effort to slow up. Both continued with undiminished speed. Then Sir Grummore rammed his head against the beech in which Wart was sitting, and King Pellinore collided with a chestnut at the other side of the clearing. The trees shook, the forest rang. Blackbirds and squirrels cursed and wood-pigeons flew out of their leafy perches half a mile away. The two knights stood to attention while one could count three. Then, with a last unanimous melodious clang, they both fell prostrate on the fatal sward.

"Stunned," said Merlyn, "I should think."

"Oh, dear," said the Wart. "Ought we to get down and help them?"

"We could pour water on their heads," said Merlyn reflectively, "if there was any water. But I don't suppose they would thank us for making their armour rusty. They will be all right. Besides, it is time that we were home."

"But they might be dead!"

"They are not dead, I know. In a minute or two they will come round and go off home to dinner."

"Poor King Pellinore has not got a home."

"Then Sir Grummore will invite him to stay the night. They will be the best of friends when they come to. They always are."

TH White

The Sword in the Stone

Display a picture of two knights squabbling, with speech bubbles.

PSHE and citizenship learning objectives

◆ To recognise mistakes and make amends when they have fallen out with friends and family (1b).

◆ To realise the consequences of aggressive behaviour (2c).

◆ To resolve differences by looking at alternatives, making decisions and explaining choices (2f).

◆ To be aware of different types of relationship, including those between friends, and to develop the skills to be effective in relationships (4c).

◆ To realise the nature and consequences of aggressive behaviours, and how to respond to them and ask for help (4d).

Background notes

This version of the Arthurian legend was written in the mid-20th century. The setting and vocabulary can be difficult, but it is worth introducing to Year 5 and 6 children and confident readers in Year 4.

Vocabulary

Fight, squabble, opponent, cheat, name call, pax, cad, yield, compromise, bicker.

Discussing the text

◆ Read the introduction then the first part of the text, up to the second *"Yes, you did"*, and go over any unusual vocabulary. Why did Wart think King Pellinore was a cheat? (He said he wanted peace then changed his mind when his opponent relaxed and then he struck him when the man wasn't ready or expecting it.) Do the children agree it was cheating? (They may think that tricks are okay in fighting. Develop the morality of fair combat if so.)

◆ What will happen now? If it doesn't emerge from suggestions, ask if these two are now going to fight more seriously and with more anger?

◆ Read the next section to *thundering together like two runaway trams*. Again help with the language. What happened? (They began to squabble rather than fight most of the time.) Have the children ever got involved in a kind of squabble like this (for example, *You did / I did not!*)? Are they being silly? (They are arguing about nothing.) Explain that sometimes we get locked into squabbles with friends or family about silly things. We won't give up, nor will our opposition. We end up getting more and more angry and sometimes fighting or falling out with our friends or family.

◆ Ask: *How do we know that these two knights are not serious enemies?* (When King Pellimore had the advantage and threatened to cut the knight's head off he didn't go through with it. He didn't want to kill Sir Grunmore.) Can the children remember a time when they have tried to make someone do something by threatening them and they wouldn't co-operate, then, because they didn't want to hurt their friend, they ended up pleading with him or her to give in, like the King did? Explain that threats and force don't always work, particularly with someone you are friendly with. Responding by simply agreeing to disagree might end the trouble.

◆ Ask the children if these two knights are now no longer going to be friends? After all they have hurt one another by calling each other names and fighting one another. Read the last part of the extract and ask the children if Merlyn was right about the knights staying friends. What lesson did Wart learn from watching these knights squabbling? (Not to fight over silly things, don't cheat, don't name-call.)

◆ Do the children think the knights enjoyed their squabbling and fighting? If so, why? Explain that sometimes we quite enjoy rowing which is strange. This is sometimes because rowing can increase adrenalin and make us feel excited and powerful. It also allows us to 'let off steam'. Meeting the challenge of matching an argument can also be fun.

PSHE and citizenship activities

◆ Ask the children to write a story about two friends squabbling and falling out over something silly, because neither would yield. Tell them to swap their stories with partners, asking what the two characters should have done to prevent the falling out. (Compromise.)

◆ In pairs, get the children to role-play a conversation between Wart and Merlyn as they watch the knights squabbling and fighting. What does Wart think about what he is seeing? How does Merlyn explain it? Ask the children to act out their scenes in turn within a group of six, then, as a group, write down what is wrong with the squabbling and fighting in Wart's view. (The bickering was over silly, unimportant things, not anything that really mattered. Then this degenerated into bad feeling and more serious fighting. It wasn't how good friends should behave.)

◆ Using the story as an example, ask the children to decide, in small groups, the point when playful bickering turns into something serious. What tips playful squabbling into something far more hurtful and damaging? (Usually something personal is said that hurts or it becomes physical, one or both loses their temper.) Encourage the children to come up with some fair-play 'rules for engagement' for those who enjoy a squabble, but don't want to spoil their friendship. Let them word-process these for display.

◆ Ask the children to imagine Wart intervened in the squabble. What did he say to help resolve the conflict and what happened after that? Tell them to write Wart's diary account of the incident.

◆ How can a friend or bystander stop a squabble between friends becoming hurtful? In pairs, ask the children to come up with some suggestions, for example asking them to stop being so stupid or nasty, making a joke to break up the tension, suggesting they all do something else like play football, and share them with the class. Then get the whole class to agree upon some useful ways of stopping squabbling and fighting between family and friends. Publish these on the computer for display.

Further literacy ideas

◆ Identify some of the archaic words used in the text. Why has the writer used these? (To convey the medieval setting.) Get the children to produce a glossary for use with the text. The children could then find other examples of historical novels that use archaic language.

◆ Examine the bickering conversation in the extract. How has the author speeded up the dialogue? (By avoiding *he said, he answered* and so on.) What are the dangers of this? (You can get confused about who is saying what.) In pairs, ask the children to write their own squabble dialogue in the style of TH White, using speech marks and correct punctuation. Tell them to read it through aloud, taking a part each. If it seems to work, let them record the dialogue on a tape recorder, ensuring that emotion is put into the voice and the speech is clear.

◆ Ask the children to write a poem about a squabble that went wrong. Tell them: *Imagine your best friend is no longer your friend. Write about your feelings and regrets.*

E-mail quarrel

*Two friends regularly send
each other e-mail messages
as well as play together
in the playground and
visit one another's houses.*

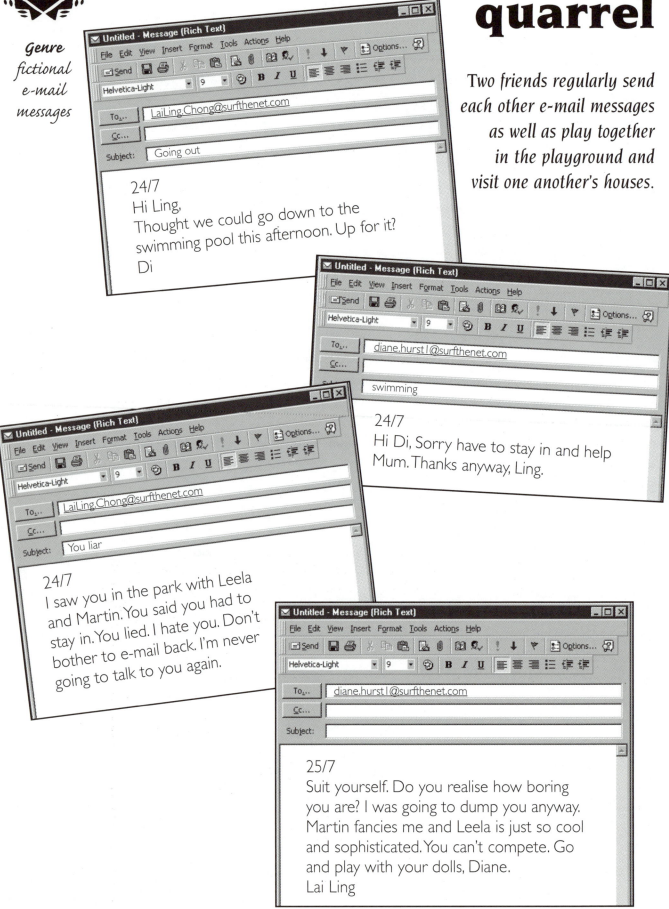

Untitled - Message (Rich Text)

To... LaiLing.Chong@surfthenet.com
Cc...
Subject: Going out

24/7
Hi Ling,
Thought we could go down to the swimming pool this afternoon. Up for it?
Di

Untitled - Message (Rich Text)

To... diane.hurst1@surfthenet.com
Cc...
swimming

24/7
Hi Di, Sorry have to stay in and help Mum. Thanks anyway, Ling.

Untitled - Message (Rich Text)

To... LaiLing.Chong@surfthenet.com
Cc...
Subject: You liar

24/7
I saw you in the park with Leela and Martin. You said you had to stay in. You lied. I hate you. Don't bother to e-mail back. I'm never going to talk to you again.

Untitled - Message (Rich Text)

To... diane.hurst1@surfthenet.com
Cc...
Subject:

25/7
Suit yourself. Do you realise how boring you are? I was going to dump you anyway. Martin fancies me and Leela is just so cool and sophisticated. You can't compete. Go and play with your dolls, Diane.
Lai Ling

E-mail quarrel

Display printed e-mail messages and replies; rules for communicating when at fault or when hurt.

PSHE and citizenship learning objectives

◆ To recognise mistakes and to make amends when they have fallen out with friends (1b).

◆ To resolve differences by looking at alternatives, making decisions and explaining choices (2f).

◆ To be aware of different types of relationship including those between friends, and to develop the skills to be effective in relationships (4c).

◆ To realise the consequences of deception on friends.

◆ To realise that communication, conciliation and honesty can help preserve friendships.

◆ To recognise the value of having many friends rather than just one.

Vocabulary

E-mail, friend, betrayal, dump, sophisticated, retaliation, communication, honesty.

Discussing the text

◆ Read through the introduction and then the e-mail messages in sequence. Make sure the children understand what an e-mail message is, how it is sent and the format it takes.

◆ Ask the children who they think is at fault and why. (Probably Lai Ling for lying, but Diane didn't help the matter by being so swift in ending the friendship.)

◆ Discuss Lai Ling's actions in lying and arranging to meet someone else. Why was that wrong? Might there have been a reasonable explanation? (For example, she had previously arranged to go out with Martin and Leela and didn't want to hurt Diane's feelings by telling her that.)

◆ Do best friends have to go out only with each other? (No. Having lots of friends is the best way, rather than just one special friend with whom you spend all your spare time. Sometimes, when you spend all your time with just one person you start to get on each other's nerves or bore one another.)

◆ Did Diane and Lai Ling mean all they said in their last e-mails? (Probably not, but each of them wanted to hurt her friend for hurting her.) Explain that this is retaliation and it only makes things worse. Letting the person know that you have been hurt and made angry is the right way of approaching this, not hurting back.

◆ Read this alternative e-mail that might have been sent to Diane after the *You liar* message:

Diane, I'm sorry. I didn't think you'd see us. We'd arranged to go out earlier and I didn't want to hurt your feelings. Please forgive me. I do want to stay your friend because I enjoy your company, but I do understand if you don't want that,
Lai Ling.

Ask the children if that would have changed the outcome. Allow a free range of ideas here. How would Diane reply? Get the class to decide on a response that you record on the board. How has Diane helped herself stay friends with Lai Ling? Record the children's ideas, which should include admitting fault, explaining honestly, apologising, expressing the desire to stay friends, acknowledging that Diane might not accept that.

PSHE and citizenship activities

◆ In pairs, ask the children to write an alternative set of e-mail messages from the moment Diane discovered that Lai Ling was in the park. Explain that, in this case, both Diane and Lai Ling are going to do their best to keep the friendship.

◆ Divide the class into two, asking half to write a diary entry as Lai Ling after she has received the *You liar* message. How does she feel? What can she do? The other half should write Diane's diary entry for the same night.

◆ Ask pairs of children to write up a series of principles for making amends when you've upset or done something wrong to your friend. Then tell them to write up a series of principles for the friend who's been hurt to follow.

◆ Discuss why betrayal of friendship is so bad an act. Why does it hurt so much? (It breaks trust and makes you feel unloved and uncared for.) What can you do if you no longer get on or enjoy being with a friend? (Tell them as kindly as possible that you want to have a rest from the friendship for a while, or make sure you are always doing things with a group of friends in which that friend is a part.)

◆ Ask the children to write a story about two best friends who fall out, but find that they miss each other's company. How do they get back together?

◆ Ask the children to write an instructional poem about how to be a good friend. What must good friends do and what must they not do?

Further literacy ideas

◆ Look at the way the e-mail messages change as the two girls get annoyed with each other. How can we tell they are angry apart from the words used? (No greeting, no sign off, short sentences, sometimes incomplete sentences.) In pairs, ask the children to write an angry exchange in e-mail format, using these ideas. Then tell them to work together to resolve their conflict. How can they change the tone of their e-mails? What should they say (and how)? Encourage them *both* to apologise.

◆ Tell the children to look up the meanings of *sophisticated* and *conciliation* and find out what they mean. Write a sentence for each, using the word in a correct context.

◆ If possible, pair those children with access to e-mail at home with those without. Let them send messages, for example about school and leisure interests, once a day for five days, using the class computer and school e-mail. At the end of five days, print and display the messages.

◆ Compare the conventions for writing e-mail with letters. Establish that messages are often quite short (partly because replies can be received quickly), less rigidly structured, tend to use *Hi* or *Hello* rather than the formal *Dear*, the e-mail address can be automatically included, they tend to be written in a more note-style form. Compared to letters, e-mails can be more active rather than reflective, and functional rather than discursive, particularly when used to arrange a meeting or a night out, for example. However, e-mails are increasingly replacing letters in a less functional context. Ask the children if any of them occasionally send long, chatty e-mails to tell their news to friends or relatives.

◆ What are the advantages of e-mail communication over direct speech or letters? What are the disadvantages? Ask the children to write these on a divided piece of paper. At the bottom of the paper, see if they can identify a situation for which these forms would be best used.

How to be a peacemaker

Genre
advisory
instructions

Offering to help
● If you spot a dispute in its early stages go and offer to help. If help is rejected, walk away but get a teacher or welfare assistant to help.
● If opponents start fighting, get an adult immediately.

Helping
● Ask the two opponents to go somewhere quiet to talk this through away from the friends.
● Make sure both opponents agree to listen to each other and keep insisting upon this.
● Ask each opponent to explain what the dispute was about.
● Summarise the problem from both points of view.
● Ask each opponent how they feel about what has happened.
● Ask each opponent what they want.
● Ask the two opponents to come up with some compromise solution that both can agree upon.
● If that fails and the two opponents don't want to forget it, ask an adult to intervene.

Follow up
Keep an eye on the two opponents in case the dispute flares up again. Report to an adult if this happens.

How to be a peacemaker

Display the text and playscripts incorporating the use of these instructions in its action.

PSHE and citizenship learning objectives

◆ To face new challenges positively by collecting information, looking for help, making responsible choices, and taking action (1c).
◆ To realise that there are different kinds of responsibilities to keep and help make peace (2d).
◆ To resolve differences by looking at alternatives, making decisions and explaining choices (2f)
◆ To recognise the different risks in different situations and then decide how to behave responsibly, judging what is acceptable and unacceptable (3e).

Background notes

These are instructions for mediation in disputes. The context is between children in school, but the instructions can be adapted for other situations.

Vocabulary

Mediator, peacemaker, compromise, opponent, dispute.

Discussing the text

◆ Read the title with the children and ask them what a peacemaker is. Who is the audience of this text? (Children who want to be peacemakers.) What type of text is it? (Instructional.) Where and when would this text be used, or put into action? (The playground, though it could be used anywhere, when a row breaks out.)
◆ Read the section 'Offering to help'. Ask the children how they would know that a row was breaking out. (There would be raised voices, sharp words, nasty words, a crowd gathering.) What are the problems of getting involved in an argument like this? (You could be drawn in and end up making things worse, the opponents could turn on you.) Ask the children if it is better to ignore the dispute or offer help? (This will depend on the situation, and a potential peacemaker would need to judge it carefully.)

◆ Ask two confident children to come out and role-play a simple dispute. Explain that one says the other tripped him up deliberately when he was running past, the other says he didn't. Read the next section – 'Helping' and work through the instructions with the children. Why is it important to get both people to listen to one another? (They need to know how the other person sees the problem. The problem can't be solved if the opponents don't acknowledge each other's views.) With you acting as mediator, enact this part with the two disputants.
◆ The peacemaker or mediator is expected to sum up the problem. How does this help? (It makes it clear.) Enact this part with the two volunteers.

◆ The mediator asks for the opponents to say how they feel. Why does she do this? (To give each a chance to say how hurt or angry they are.) Enact the scene.

◆ Finally, the mediator asks what each wants and calls for some agreed compromise position. This puts an end to the dispute and lets each opponent solve the problems themselves rather than rely on an adult to decide the solution. Role-play this scene.

◆ Read the final section with the children. Why does the mediator need to keep an eye on the opponents? (Sometimes, their feelings re-emerge and they want to fight.)

◆ Ask the children how this mediation role is different to a teacher's or welfare assistant's role. (There is no judgement or telling off. The mediator is not in a more powerful position than the opponents.)

◆ Do the children think this might help people in the playground? Accept a range of views, but ask them to justify their reasoning without making personal comments.

PSHE and citizenship activities

◆ Ask the children to write a short story where a dispute breaks out between two children. No one stops it and it ends up in a fight. Both are hurt and both are in serious trouble. What happens and how do they each feel?

◆ Ask the children to make notes for a drama about a situation in the playground when a dispute between two people breaks out. In threes, ask them to role-play the scenarios, taking turns to mediate in their own created dispute. Encourage them to identify problems and successes and work out as a group how to overcome the problems using the instructions. Ask the groups to perform their scenes to the class. You could then set up regular practice sessions on how to mediate and children can begin to internalise the process.

◆ Discuss with the whole class whether they would like to try and put the peacemaker scheme into operation in the school. Who should be the peacemakers, what should they be called, how should they be identified (badges, sweatshirts of special colour)? Should there be a pilot scheme? How can it be organised? Who needs to be informed? (Parents, children, welfare assistance, teachers.) If the children do not want to take part or think it will fail then leave it or consider it for another class.

◆ Discuss with the children if they think this technique would be useful at home. Could they use it to intervene between their siblings and their friends, or amongst their own friends out of school? Could the children eventually be able to resolve their own disputes without a mediator? Suggest that this is the ideal to work towards.

◆ Ask a police officer to come in and talk about how they mediate in disputes and how important it is to solve problems without resorting to violence.

Further literacy ideas

◆ Ask the children to write an instructional text in this format for accessing the computer software programmes or for tackling a problem with their schoolwork.

◆ Ask the children to provide simple working definitions for the words *mediation*, *conciliation* and *pilot scheme*, checking their work in a dictionary.

◆ The children could write a letter to parents or teachers, or welfare assistants, explaining the mediation pilot scheme and how it will work. Encourage the children to address any concerns they think the adults may have.

◆ In small groups, let the children brainstorm a range of names for this scheme. Advise them that the name should indicate the idea of the scheme in a simple word or phrase. Using the ideas generated, vote as a class for the best name to adopt.

Keeping safe and healthy

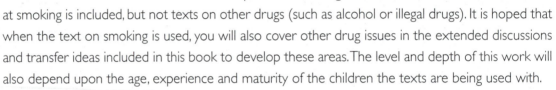

Keeping safe and healthy within the context of PSHE at Key Stage 2, revolves around various themes and has strong links with the science curriculum. There are many areas of possible focus within this section, but unfortunately not all can be covered in this chapter. It is intended that you will extend the work started from the texts into broader areas through expanding the discussion of the issues raised. For example, a text looking at smoking is included, but not texts on other drugs (such as alcohol or illegal drugs). It is hoped that when the text on smoking is used, you will also cover other drug issues in the extended discussions and transfer ideas included in this book to develop these areas. The level and depth of this work will also depend upon the age, experience and maturity of the children the texts are being used with.

Much of the content of this chapter will already be part of schools' medium-term planning for health education and will have been happening in a variety of ways for a number of years. The texts chosen are intended to augment this work already in place.

The texts have been deliberately chosen to suit most children in the Key Stage 2 age range, but for some older children, you may feel that they can go into greater detail in some subjects. Much of the work started in this chapter will be an introduction for work which will continue well into Key Stages 3 and 4, and it is important that, although we give children information to help them make informed decisions and look after themselves, we don't scare them or, at the other extreme, encourage them to experiment.

The main focus of this chapter is to encourage children to reflect on their lifestyle and to make healthier lifestyle choices. Children are encouraged to consider what they eat, how they keep fit, what benefits exercise has on their bodies, what things are harmful to their bodies and to understand that people need to look after their bodies if they are to continue to work efficiently.

It is also important that children know how to keep safe and cultivate the skills of risk assessment. This will enable them to make informed choices about their actions and understand the impact of peer pressure on the behaviour of children.

The work within this chapter also encourages children to seek appropriate help through a variety of agencies, and there are many opportunities to invite visitors into school to talk to the children about their work and the contribution this makes society. Many of the topics included are also well covered by voluntary organisations who can supply leaflets, advice and even visitors. Tacade (www.tacade.com) produce wonderful drug education material, and the British Heart Foundation (www.bhf.org.uk) have a wide and varied range of material about looking after our hearts and bodies.

Lastly, the activities help to make children aware of health and safety procedures in school and to learn first aid, emergency resuscitation and fire safety in the home.

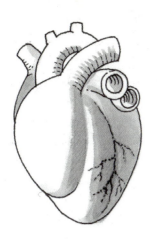

The way to a healthy heart is through the stomach

Genre
information leaflet for children, with diagrams and tables

When we talk about healthy eating we don't mean going on some kooky 'nothing but lettuce for a whole week' kind of deal. We just mean the way you eat in general. It's all about finding a balance.

You need to watch all those yummy foods you know are high in fat and get into the more natural ones.

Fresh fruits, veggies, even fish and chicken are perfect. That's not to say you can't indulge, it's just that you can't live, literally, on biscuits and sweets.

It's a bummer but that's life. So as you start keeping an eye on what you eat try this little quiz on your parents. It's a blast. Next time they're unpacking the shopping read some of the labels and start casually asking questions like:

■ "What percentage of saturated fat is in that margarine?"

■ "How many calories in that pie comes from fat?"

■ "Is that milk skimmed or semi-skimmed?"

Then you quiz them on the recommended daily intakes for the most important nutrients listed on food labels.

Text © British Heart Foundation

Men		Women
95g	Fat	70g
2.5g	Sodium	2g
70g	Sugar	50g
20g	Fibre	16g

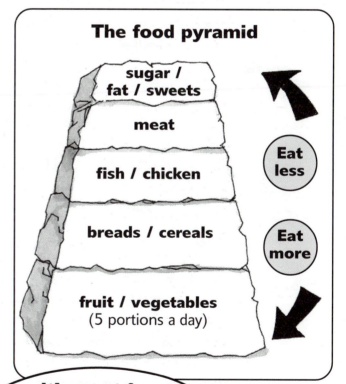

The food pyramid

sugar / fat / sweets

meat

fish / chicken

breads / cereals

fruit / vegetables
(5 portions a day)

Eat less

Eat more

It's great fun showing your parents they don't know everything! And you'll learn a few things along the way.

The way to a healthy heart is through the stomach

Display a collection of texts and leaflets about healthy eating and a range of packets and tins and labels of food. Include on the display vocabulary for the topic, for example *carbohydrate*, *protein*, *food group* and so on.

PSHE and citizenship learning objectives

◆ To recognise the role of voluntary, community and pressure groups (2h).

◆ To know what makes a healthy lifestyle, including the benefits of exercise and healthy eating (3a).

◆ To recognise that differences and similarities between people arise from a number of factors, including gender (4f).

◆ To feel positive about themselves by being in control of a healthy diet and a healthy heart (5b).

◆ To make real choices and decisions about issues affecting their health (5d).

Background notes

From PSHE lessons in Key Stage 1, children should be aware of the basic food groups we eat and what sorts of food belong in each group. If they need reminding, see the chapter on Keeping healthy in *Teaching with text: PSHE and citizenship ages 5–7*. You may want to explain or revise that the heart is a muscle which continually pumps blood around the body, delivering oxygen from the lungs to all parts of the body and removing waste products.

Vocabulary

Protein, carbohydrate, fats, sugar, healthy, heart, blast, kooky, intake, balance, saturated fat, skimmed, nutrients.

Discussing the text

◆ Before reading the text, remind the children that the food we eat can be sorted into different food groups. Some are better for us than others. Which?

◆ Look at the food pyramid diagram. What message is this diagram giving us? Ask the children to give examples of each type of food listed. What should we eat more of? What should we eat less of? Which types of food do the children prefer to eat?

◆ Now read the whole text with the children. What are the main messages in the text? It isn't written in a conventional style, so summarise with the children the main themes of the text in more standard English.

◆ Look at the recommended intakes of fat, sodium, sugar and fibre for an adult man and woman. What do the children notice? Why are there differences? Do they think there will be differences for children too? (They are different for men, women and children because of weight, height and body composition.)

◆ Look at some of the more unusual words in the text, for example *kooky* and *blast*. Discuss with the children what they mean. Explore the fact that words can change, depending on the context in which they are used, for example *blast* (normally an explosion; here a lot of fun).

◆ Look at the layout of the text – headings, diagrams, different typefaces and sizes and so on. Discuss how this catches people's eyes and makes sure the information gets across as clearly and memorably as possible.

PSHE and citizenship activities

◆ Make a collection of packets, tins, labels and so on, of food we regularly like to eat. Ask the children to help you sort them into healthy and less healthy options and display them in the classroom.

◆ In groups, ask the children to use the collection of food packaging to find out which has the least percentage of saturated fats, how many calories come from fat and so on. Help them to make graphs to show the results and write a report to recommend which foods we can eat regularly and which we need to be more careful about. Display these with the packets.

◆ Investigate why saturated fat is not so good for us and what are the risks if we eat too much of it. Try www.bhf.org.uk/education or local and school libraries for information.

◆ Let the children write to the British Heart Foundation (at 14 Fitzhardinge Street, London W1H 6DH) or visit the website to find out what the recommended daily intakes of food types are for children. There is a special section on the site for children up to 11 years old and also a section for ordering teachers' resources.

◆ Let the children keep a weekly log of all the food they eat. Ask pairs of children to look at each other's lists and consider if they are very healthy, reasonably healthy or unhealthy. Ask them to devise an action plan to make their diets healthy. Remind them that this has to be achievable and sensible, so cutting sweets out altogether is not going to be difficult and probably won't happen, whereas having something sweet to eat only once a day may be achievable.

◆ Ask the children to try to keep to their healthy eating plan for a week and keep a diary about how it felt to do this.

◆ The children could design a healthy eating poster or leaflet for the children in a younger class.

◆ If you have a school tuck shop or school snacks, write a class letter to whoever runs it, suggesting ways of providing a healthy selection. Children could get involved in the ordering and stocking of healthy options and make posters to encourage other children to buy the healthy options.

◆ In cookery sessions, make some healthy-option biscuits, some recipes using fruit and so on and encourage the children to take the recipes home.

◆ Tell the children that another way to a healthy heart is through exercise. Investigate heart rates before and after exercise such as running round the playground, hopping, skipping. Show the children how to find a pulse and how to measure pulse rate and ask everyone to record their findings. Suggest that the children design a keep-fit regime, practise it and test their pulse rate again later in the term to see if they have managed any improvements through doing more regular exercise.

Further literacy ideas

◆ Make a collection of leaflets. Look at the layout and design of these. Can the children spot similarities? Which works best? Why? The children could then go on to make a guide to producing leaflets or posters for other children to use.

◆ Let the children use a dictionary to check the meanings of words in the context of the text and otherwise, for example *blast* and *veggies*. Then ask them to use a thesaurus to choose different words that would have a similar effect in the text.

◆ Ask the children to use the computer to experiment with different fonts, finding out which ones are most eye-catching, easiest to read and so on. Which colours on which backgrounds stand out more? This information could be included in the guide to poster/leaflet making.

Genre
rhyming poem with a refrain and rap-style rhythm; persuasive text

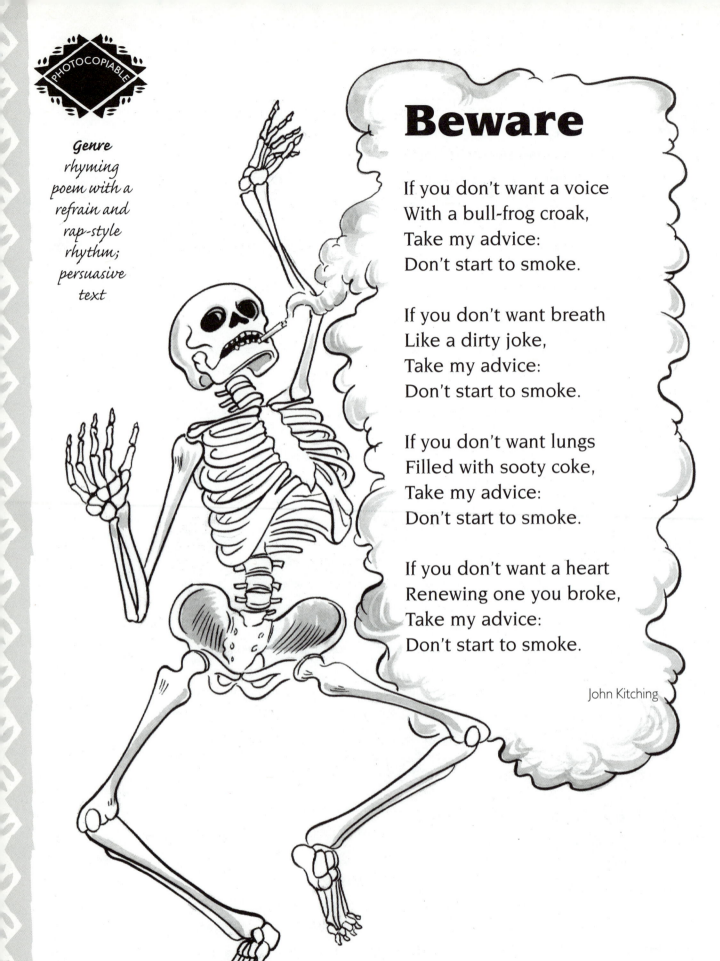

Beware

If you don't want a voice
With a bull-frog croak,
Take my advice:
Don't start to smoke.

If you don't want breath
Like a dirty joke,
Take my advice:
Don't start to smoke.

If you don't want lungs
Filled with sooty coke,
Take my advice:
Don't start to smoke.

If you don't want a heart
Renewing one you broke,
Take my advice:
Don't start to smoke.

John Kitching

Hack!

Why doesn't the government ban smoking? Is it because...?

Genre
discussion
text

☐ The government takes £9000000000 a year in taxes on cigarettes.

☐ It's your business if you smoke.

☐ They'd be voted out if they tried.

☐ Smokers who die young don't draw pensions.

☐ Many politicians smoke.

☐ Some politicians are paid huge amounts of money by tobacco companies to stop tough laws being passed.

☐ A ban would make smoking more exciting.

☐ People who work for tobacco companies, or sell tobacco products, would be out of a job.

☐ Criminals would push tobacco alongside heroin and cocaine.

I agree ☑

I disagree ☒

Do **you** think the government ought to ban smoking?

Text © British Heart Foundation

'Beware' and 'Hack!'

Display a collection of cigarette adverts and packets, and leaflets explaining about smoking and the harm it can cause.

PSHE and citizenship learning objectives

◆ To face new challenges positively, making responsible choices (1c).

◆ To research, debate and discuss topical issues (2a).

◆ To recognise the role of voluntary, community and pressure groups (2h).

◆ To explore how the media present information (2k).

◆ To know what makes a healthy lifestyle and how to make informed choices (3a).

◆ To know which commonly available substances are legal and illegal, their effects and risks (3d).

◆ To make real choices and decisions about issues affecting their health and well-being (5d).

Background notes

These texts are useful in taking different approaches to the topic of smoking. The poem is trying to persuade the reader not to smoke and the extract from 'Hack!' (one section from an A–Z leaflet on smoking published by the British Heart Foundation in 1998) opens a debate on one societal aspect of smoking. The second piece is more appropriate for Years 5 and 6, but the poem and some of the activities can be used with Years 3 to 6. Children of all ages are aware of smokers, especially in their families, and open and honest discussion may help to prevent them smoking when they're older, when they will be able to make informed decisions.

Vocabulary

Cigarette, smoking, lungs, harmful, nicotine, taking a risk, passive smoking, habit, addiction, drug.

Discussing the texts

◆ First, read the poem with the children. Try to get the rap-type rhythm going.

◆ Discuss with the children the main theme of the poem. What is it? What is the poem telling us not to do? Should poets be able to tell us what to do?

◆ Discuss what smoking is. Why do people smoke? Do the children have anyone in their family that smokes? What do they think of smoking? You could discuss here the historical fact that, at one time, people didn't think that smoking was bad for you. Now we know that smoking can contribute to an early death, but some people accept that and take the risk.

◆ Is the poem accurate about the things smoking can do to us? Discuss what each verse is suggesting. Do the children agree with the experience of the poet?

◆ Talk about what lungs are, what they look like (try to get a picture or model to illustrate this) and what they do. Then discuss what effect smoking has on the lungs and why this makes smoking harmful. Also discuss the fact that people can be passive smokers. The children may be aware of adults who smoke near them. Encourage them to move away or not to stay in smoky places.

◆ Now look at 'Hack!'. Go through the statements with the children, making sure they understand everything. At this point, don't discuss whether they agree or not.

◆ Ask the children in pairs to decide if they think the statements are true or false, feeding back to the rest of the class. Explain that there is no right or wrong answer – it will depend on opinion.

PSHE and citizenship activities

◆ Show the children a collection of cigarette adverts from magazines, newspapers and on things like formula one racing cars. Ask the children to consider the feel of the adverts. What are they trying to portray? What image are they giving smoking? Do the children think that the adverts tempt people to buy cigarettes? Where is the government health warning? How big is it? In groups, ask the children to write a magazine article debating the pros and cons of advertising.

◆ Investigate the facts about smoking and the harm it can do. Why do people take up smoking? Why do they continue? (Include the terms *habit* and *addiction* in this discussion.) Are there any advantages for being a smoker? Help the children to write a factual report about smoking without a bias.

◆ Look at the responses to the questionnaire. What do they tell us? Is there a consensus for a government ban? Each child should form their own opinion through this discussion. Ask individuals to write a letter to the local MP, supporting smoking in public, private places only, or supporting the ban.

◆ To investigate in a shocking but effective way the harm cigarettes can do, you could demonstrate what happens by using a large plastic drinks bottle half filled with cotton wool, the neck plugged with a bung with a hole in it for a cigarette. Light the cigarette and 'smoke' it by carefully squeezing the bottle. The cotton wool, which represents the lungs, will soon become black and gooey with nicotine and tar. Ask the children to imagine that if this is what one cigarette does, what about several a day for years? Make sure you practise this experiment first and follow all safety procedures.

◆ Look at statistics of smoking related diseases. These can be accessed from various websites and leaflets. You could try www.ash.org.uk (a site for adults, but with useful information) or www.bhf.org.uk/education. (Order the leaflet 'Hack!' – it has some wonderful facts and interesting information on it.)

◆ Consider no-smoking signs. What do they look like? Where are they found? Why is smoking not allowed in some places? Ask the children to design their own no-smoking signs.

◆ Talk about making sensible choices and informed decisions. In groups, ask the children to produce little plays showing children trying to persuade other children to smoke. Look at the options available to people put under pressure from their peers. How could they make the right choice for themselves?

◆ Explore the wider issues of taking other drugs. Stress the importance of making informed decisions. You may wish to discuss the use of alcohol by adults in limited amounts, often in a social context. Help the children to find information about other types of drugs and set up similar investigations. For example, certain drugs are needed when people are very ill and in pain, but when used by other people, they can be harmful. Explain that some drugs are thought to be so dangerous that they are illegal. Remind the children that they should never take medicine prescribed for someone else.

◆ Consider the use of drugs to keep people well and explain that some people must take drugs as medicine to stay well, for example asthma or epilepsy sufferers, diabetics and so on. If appropriate, ask if there are any children in the class who would share their experiences of these conditions and help others to become more aware of them.

Further literacy ideas

◆ Look at the characteristics of persuasive texts. Ask the children to write a piece of text persuading someone to give up smoking. This could be in a variety of forms, for example a poster or a letter.

◆ Let the children try writing their own poem about smoking in the style of the poem 'Beware'. Remind them to use the poet's final two lines of each verse.

◆ Ask the children to write an acrostic poem about smoking.

◆ Tell the children to create a story about a child who is egged onto smoke or drink and refuses. What pressures does she or he feel? What does she say and do?

Get out, get the brigade out...
stay out!

Few things are more frightening than a fire in your home. One day it could happen to you.

If there is a fire in your home, it will be much easier for you to escape if you have already thought about the best way to get out.

Why not talk about your escape route with Mum, Dad or another adult where you live? And draw an escape plan.

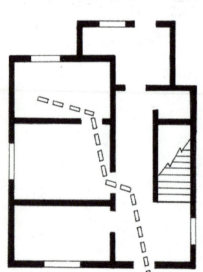

Make sure you have worked out your escape route in advance.

Once you have worked out your escape route, make sure you always keep it clear of toys and other things that could block your way out.

Suppose a fire has started in your home and you discover it. What do you do?

1. Raise the alarm. Tell an adult.
2. Get out. Get others out, too, if you can. But don't risk your own life.
3. Get the brigade out. Go to the nearest telephone outside your house, dial **999** and ask for the fire brigade. (The nearest telephone might be a neighbour's, or it could be a phone box.)

4. Stay out. Don't go back in for anything. Your life is much more precious than your toys, or even your pets.

If your clothes catch fire...

1. **Stop**. Don't run, as this will make the fire worse.
2. **Drop**. Get down on the floor.
3. **Roll** over, as this will put the flames out. Keep on rolling until it does.

It's far better, of course, to stop fires starting at all. Here are a few fire prevention tips:
❑ Don't play with matches.
❑ Don't stand or play too close to fires or heaters.
❑ Don't leave toys or clothes on, or too close to, fires and heaters.
❑ Unplug anything electrical that you have been using. Not every appliance is designed to be left switched on all the time. Play it safe: unplug it.

A bedtime routine
Ask yourself:
❑ Is my escape route clear?
❑ Have I switched everything off?

Get out, get the brigade out... stay out!

Display books and posters about the fire brigade and other emergency services, fire exit signs, fire procedure posters and instructions as displayed around school and other public places, a smoke alarm, a fire extinguisher.

PSHE and citizenship learning objectives

◆ To know about the range of jobs carried out by people they know and to understand how they can develop skills to make their own contribution in the future (1e).

◆ To recognise the different risks in different situations and then decide how to behave responsibly (3e).

◆ To know the school rules about health and safety, basic emergency aid procedures and where to get help (3g).

◆ To meet and talk with people who work in the school and neighbourhood (5e).

Background notes

This text is from a Home Office 'Play it Safe Action for Child Safety' leaflet. You may wish to tackle this text in two halves, as there is a lot of information for younger children to take in all at once.

Vocabulary

Safety, smoke alarm, fire alarm, procedure, flammable, inflammable, escape route.

Discussing the text

◆ Read the text through in sections, discussing with the children each point as it is made. First, discuss the possibility of fire at home. Look at the plan together. Explain what a plan shows and the symbols used, for example for doors, window, and stairs. Many children will not have seen a plan drawn in this way and will need help interpreting it. What sorts of things do we need to consider when planning an escape route? (For example, a window onto a garage roof, a window big enough to climb out of. Do the children know where this is in their home?) Suggest that a window that opens above a hard surface will be less safe than above grass. When could we use the stairs? How close to the stairs is the front door? Which would be the best exit – the front door or the back?

◆ Discuss what to do if a fire starts in the home. What does *Raise the alarm* mean? Talk about the alarms in school. What are they? Where are they? Do the children have them at home? (Smoke alarms probably, but it's unlikely that a home has a fire alarm. Children who live in flats, however, should know about any fire alarms in the communal areas of their buildings.) Discuss what the phrase means in this context. Ask the children what they would they do to raise the alarm.

◆ What do the children feel about the final statement in this section: *Your life is much more precious than your toys, or even your pets?* This may lead to quite an in-depth discussion. Why shouldn't they go back even if it looks safe? What may happen? Discuss the nature of fire being spread by draughts, building up behind doors and then bursting out when they are opened, appliances heating up and exploding, structures collapsing and so on.

◆ Go through the instructions for what to do if your clothes catch fire and let children practise the procedure in a hall time.

◆ Look at the prevention tips and bedtime routine. Discuss what *prevention* means. Look at the last of the four tips. Is it realistic these days to unplug everything? What about the fridge, and computers, bedside lights, television and audio equipment? Discuss that some things are designed to be left on standby, but others are not. Which appliances is it sensible to unplug or switch off at the socket? (For example, the vacuum cleaner, the iron, the kettle, the toaster.)

PSHE and citizenship activities

◆ Ask the children to work out at home what would be the best exit routes if a fire started upstairs or downstairs and to draw an action plan as in the text. Suggest that they take it home for everyone there to learn.

◆ In a PE session or hall time, let the children practise the routine for when clothes catch fire so they are familiar with what to do. Let them watch each other to check they are doing it correctly.

◆ Invite a local fire officer into school to talk to the children. They may even bring a smoke tunnel with them. Ask the children to prepare questions to ask the fire officer about his or her job and how to become a firefighter. After the visit, ask the children to write about aspects of the job that particularly interested or surprised them. Would any of them like to become firefighters when they are older?

◆ If you are fortunate enough to have a smoke tunnel as part of the visit, ask the children to write a description about how it felt to be inside and how they reacted. Were any of them frightened? Were they disoriented? Did they panic a little? Discuss what implications this has for how we should behave if we were in a fire.

◆ Get the children to write their own fire code instructions for home or school.

◆ Make sure all the children know about the fire drill in school and arrange a school practice.

◆ Help the children to make a plan of where the fire alarms in school are, checking that they are easily visible and that the fire extinguishers are accessible. They could write a formal report about what they find to the headteacher and caretaker. School monitors could be appointed to check each week that all fire exit signs, extinguishers, alarms and so on are all accessible and visible.

◆ Ask the children to make list of the electrical things they have in their homes and investigate which could or should be unplugged at night. Nearly all new equipment is designed to be left safely on standby, older items probably aren't. Which things are used regularly and which less often? Establish the children's understanding of why it is dangerous to leave certain electric things on. Reinforce the dangers of electricity and how we must never poke things into plugs or sockets as they can kill.

◆ Ask the children to write about the dangers of fire in various contexts and how people should behave near fire, for example on bonfire night and when having a barbecue.

Further literacy ideas

◆ Ask the children to write an exciting story about a fire starting in a house in the middle of the night and how the family escape.

◆ Discuss with the children their experiences of fires. Have they been to a bonfire? Do they have a real fire for heating at home? Do their parents ever have a fire to burn garden waste? Ask the children to write a description of fire, vividly portraying what it looks like and smells like and how the heat it gives off feels. Encourage them to use simile and metaphor to enhance the images.

◆ Investigate the magic e rule: for short words like *fir* and *cap*, adding an e changes sound of the consonant from short to long – *fire* and *cape*.

Look before you leap

Genre
adventure story, serial

"Bored! Bored!" Jez yelled.

Leaping to his feet, the boy paced back and forth in front of the park bench, watched unhappily by his two school mates. When Jez got bored, things happened.

"I've got it!" Jez cried, his face lighting up with excitement. "Come on!" and he darted through the crowd of shoppers.

When Jez finally came to a halt, eyes shining wildly, Ajay and Paul were too breathless to quiz him. Their mums would kill them. They were supposed to stay in the park. Too late now!

The boys' worry deepened to real fear as Jez climbed up onto a high wall that bordered the railway embankment, legs straddling the thick wall top.

"We can't!" Ajay cried. "It's private! We'd be trespassing."

Jez grinned. "We're not trespassing, we're exploring."

Ajay shut his eyes in disbelief, only to snap them open again as Paul tried. "It's dangerous – look!"

All eyes diverted to the battered sign clearly saying 'Keep Out – Danger'.

"That's just to keep people out," Jez argued. "Come on."

He didn't wait any longer, but hurled himself over the edge.

Ajay and Paul had separately resolved to go no further in this escapade until a sharp cry of pain reached their ears; a shared glance and both boys were scrambling up over the wall. Unlike their friend, the two boys halted momentarily at the top, brought up on the maxim 'Look before you leap'. It was just as well, for on the railway side of the wall was a drop of some three metres to a steeply sloping bank leading down to the railway lines. There at the bottom of the bank, in a motionless, crumpled heap, was Jez.

Slithering on hands and heels, the boys reached their friend. Only when they were kneeling over the still figure did a soft, maddening laugh come from the body. Jez's face cracked into a wide grin as he sat up effortlessly, then punched the nearer of the two boys.

"Got you going there, didn't I?"

Ajay was up on his feet, fists clenched, ready to fight. Jez matched him, squaring up, with eyes glittering with expectation.

"Don't!" Paul barked out, bravely stepping between his two friends. "We're in enough trouble as it is."

"Hey! You lads!"

The sharp yell came from the direction of the wall. It had to be the police or security. All three boys hared off down the track-side.

Up by the wall, the railway security guard shouted again, radioed in to base, then clambered over the wall to give chase.

Each of the boys ran his fastest, unaware of the others. No one saw Jez fall behind as the pains in his chest got worse. He really had hurt himself when he fell. Now he couldn't breath any more. The pain worsened. With an agonising cry, he staggered to the left then tumbled into darkness.

PHOTOCOPIABLE

Paul twisted around, expecting to see Jez laughing with excitement behind him. All he saw was the boy lying on the track fifty metres back. He yelled to Ajay to stop.

"He's fooling," Ajay spat.

"No, he isn't!"

For a moment, Ajay wavered, then together the two friends ran back, straight into trouble.

A buzzing sound roused Jez from his faint, that and a powerful sense of danger.

"Don't move, Jez! Please!"

It was Ajay, a very panicky Ajay.

"Help me," Jez cried.

"I can't. The line's live, Jez. We'll get electrocuted. I think a train's coming."

This wasn't comforting Jez. If a train was coming, he had to get off that track. There were two problems to this master plan. First, Jez was terrified of frying. Second, when he tried to move, the pain in his chest stopped him dead. He was stuck.

"Get help," Jez cried.

"The woman's coming."

Jez shut his eyes and tried not to cry.

"Stay still!" came a sharp, breathless voice from somewhere above him. Jez tried to twist to see who was ordering him about. The annoying buzz grew much louder. Jez froze.

"You're centimetres from a live railway line. If you touch it, you will be killed. Do you understand?"

Jez did. "The train?" he gasped, expecting to be flattened at any moment by an Intercity and wondering at the same time if his mum would let his pain of a sister have his computer console.

The guard answered, "Stopped down the line. The current is going to be switched off soon."

For some reason, Jez shuddered, his sight blurring as the tears washed over his eyes. His pains were worse. His arms and legs seemed to want to jerk and twitch. He was panicking.

"Stay back!"

The guard's harsh order was directed at the two upset friends. They had seen Jez crying and his white face showing the terrible pain and had tried to move nearer to console him.

"I've enough trouble rescuing this idiot. I don't want three bodies to deal with."

Jez groaned but decided he'd sort this woman out later. She couldn't talk to his mates like that!

"Jez! The medics are coming."

Paul's shaky message was a great relief.

It was a kinder voice that addressed him now. "Hello Jez. I'm a paramedic. We'll get you out. You know you mustn't move, don't you?"

Contrarily, the boy nodded.

"Good lad. Where does it hurt?"

Jez found it hard to speak. Halfway through Jez's stop-start description, the paramedic interrupted him. "Hold on."

Jez scowled angrily. Who was the important one here, anyway?

The distant cold voice declared, "It's off."

There was a collective sigh of relief.

"Right, Jez," the crisp ambulance man said. "Let's get you out of there."

Gillian Goddard

Look before you leap

Display a collection of newspaper articles about people who have done stupid things, for example trespassing or stealing cars, and put themselves in grave danger as a result. Include a set of ways to refuse pressure, written in speech bubbles.

PSHE and citizenship learning objectives

◆ To be aware of the range of jobs carried out by people they know and to understand how they can develop skills to make their own contribution in the future (1e).

◆ To see that pressure to behave in an unacceptable or risky way can come from a variety of sources, including people they know (3f).

◆ To understand why and how rules and laws are made and enforced, why different rules are needed in different situations (2b).

◆ To recognise the different risks in different situations and then decide how to behave responsibly (3e).

◆ To know the school rules about health and safety, basic emergency procedure and where to get help (3g).

◆ To meet and talk with people who work in the school and neighbourhood (5e).

Background notes

This extract is from the first adventure in a series of three short stories featuring Jez and his friends. The others are included in 'Citizenship' ('Set a thief to catch a thief') and 'Relationships' ('A friend in need').

Vocabulary

Danger, trespassing, risk, paramedic, third line, electricity, irresponsible.

Discussing the text

◆ Read the story through with the class. It may be better to do this in story time the first time and then revisit the text again during the Literacy Hour to do some work on the issues it raises.

◆ Ask the children to summarise the main points of the story. Discuss who were the main characters, the setting, the plot, the conflict and resolution. What is the message the story is giving us?

◆ Discuss the 'third line' and explain what it is and why it is so dangerous. This is the electric line that provides power for the trains and has replaced overhead cables. Because it is at ground level, it is more accessible, and children need to be aware of its existence.

◆ Look at the character of Jez. What evidence is there in the text to indicate his characteristics? (He's excitable, reckless, a joker, short-tempered.) Are Ajay and Paul the same as Jez? Discuss the idea of a ringleader and what they do. Who is it in this story?

◆ The adults talked crisply and crossly to the boys. Why do the children think this was? Draw out that the boys were behaving irresponsibly, putting themselves in unnecessary danger and wasting people's time by trespassing; wasting the money involved in calling the ambulance out, preventing them from answering other calls and stopping the train and making people late.

◆ Discuss what could happen to the three boys as a result of being caught trespassing. (Their parents would be cross and may punish them, and the police may take the incident further and fine them.)

◆ Do the children think Paul, Ajay and Jez have learned a lesson? All three of them? How might they be feeling at the end of the story?

◆ Often we feel pressurised to do things we don't want to. Talk about why people can be worried about not joining in with things. What would happen? Ask the children to share experiences of times when they have said *No* and what has happened. This should illustrate that our imaginations often make us expect worse things to happen than actually do. Talk about what to do if someone is putting pressure on us to do something we don't want to. (For example, try to refuse or tell an adult.)

PSHE and citizenship activities

◆ Ask a local police officer to come in and advise the children about the dangers of the 'third line' and what accidents they have seen from people behaving irresponsibly. This will emphasise that not only do the people get hurt or even killed, but trains can be delayed or crash. Ask the children to make a poster explaining the need for safety near a railway.

◆ Find examples in the text to show how the security guard and ambulance crew felt. Ask the children to imagine they are one of the ambulance crew writing a letter to Jez that explains how he or she felt about the rescue. Encourage the children to point out that although the medic is pleased no one was hurt, there are other issues that need considering.

◆ Look at danger and warning signs. Why are they used? What sorts of places use them? What reasons do they have for using them? Help the children to realise that warning and danger signs are not there just to stop people having fun. Establish the difference between trespassing and exploring.

◆ Do the children think Ajay and Paul had the same attitude to life as Jez? What makes them think this? Before the boys went over the wall, did they all feel the same way about their 'adventure'? Ask the children to write about the decision to go over, from the point of view of Jez, Paul or Ajay.

◆ Ask the children to imagine they are Jez's family. What would they do? What mixture of feelings would they have? In groups of three, get the children to improvise the family visiting Jez in hospital.

◆ Discuss the way that Jez led the other boys into danger. Ask the children to rewrite the story from the beginning, but this time Paul and Ajay refuse to follow Jez or have anything to do with his plans or high jinks. How does this change the story?

◆ Gather a list of responses children could use when being coerced into doing something they don't want to or know is not right to do. Ask the children to write these into big speech bubbles and display them in the classroom.

Further literacy ideas

◆ The story has a successful conclusion but it could so easily have been different. Ask children to write an ending for the story where Jez is killed by the third line. Tell them to start from *A buzzing sound roused Jez from his faint, that and a powerful sense of danger…*

◆ Look at the persuasive language children use to get their friends to do what they want. Ask the children to write a poem encouraging a friend to do something that they know they shouldn't. Then, tell them to swap their poems with partners and write a poem in reply, explaining why they are not persuaded and won't do it.

◆ Ask the children to write a conversation that may have happened between the three boys in the story. Focus on the correct use of speech marks and how to use punctuation with speech.

◆ In pairs, ask the children to rewrite part of the story in the form of a play. Divide the story into specific scenes and then put all the parts together to make one whole play.

Tooth care

Genre
explanation
text

When you were born you didn't have any teeth, but as you got older they gradually grew. When you were about five or six your first teeth started to get loose and fall out and new, bigger, stronger, second teeth grew in their place. Some of you may still have some first teeth waiting to drop out. This can last until the early teens in some cases.

You only get two sets of teeth in your life and you need to look after your second teeth so that they last you until you are old and grey. Without proper care, your teeth may fall out, making food difficult to eat. You should be able to keep your teeth healthy by brushing them regularly and also by visiting your dentist every six months. The dentist will check your teeth and fix any problems before they get too serious.

Eating sweet foods causes a substance called plaque to develop in your mouth. Plaque is yellowy soft stuff that builds up on your teeth; it makes your teeth decay and this causes toothache. You may have to have fillings or, worse still, the tooth dies and falls out or has to be taken out. Plaque also causes gum disease. Brushing our teeth carefully removes this plaque from your teeth and gums and helps to keep both healthy. It is important to brush your teeth, particularly where they meet the gums, at least twice a day and especially last thing at night to stop the plaque attacking whilst you sleep. You need to use toothpaste that has fluoride in it, as this will help to make your teeth strong.

If you eat lots of sweets between meals or drink many sweet drinks without brushing your teeth, then the plaque gets to work. Try to keep sweets for meal times or try to brush your teeth after eating sweet things. This will keep the plaque away. Make sure you change your toothbrush about every three months, as worn out brushes are not as effective at removing the plaque.

Jackie Barbera

Tooth care

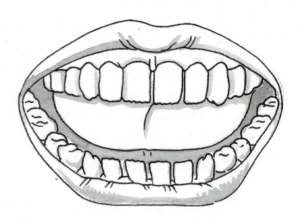

Display a large set of teeth (available from school catalogues or sometimes from the local schools' health unit), toothpaste boxes or tubes, toothbrushes, leaflets and books on teeth and dental care.

PSHE and citizenship learning objectives

◆ To know what makes a healthy lifestyle and how to make informed choices (3a).
◆ To learn that bacteria and viruses can affect health and that following simple, safe routines can reduce the spread (3b).

Vocabulary

Molars, incisors, eye teeth, flouride, plaque, bacteria, decay.

Discussing the text

◆ Read the text with the children. Discuss the main ideas and check that everyone understands all the information. Clarify some of the vocabulary that may be new.
◆ Ask the children to find out how old they were when they got their first tooth and which one it was. Also which was the first tooth they lost and when was this? Do they remember this happening? When did the children lose their last teeth?

◆ Ask who brushes their teeth regularly. What does *regularly* mean? How many times do the children brush their teeth and when? Once? Twice? After every meal? In the morning and at night? What does their mouth feel like first thing in the morning? Why is this? Talk about plaque, what it is, what it looks like, what it does. How does brushing their teeth help?

◆ Ask who visits the dentist. Ask children to share their experiences of this. At this age, most memories will be good. Emphasis the fact that if you look after your teeth, the dentist shouldn't really have to do much each time you visit.

◆ Discuss the fact that sweet things are not good for our teeth as they help plaque to spread. Why else are lots of sweet things not good for us? (They don't fill us up or give us nutrients and are fattening if we eat too many. They can even make us overactive and then lethargic.) How often do the children eat sweet things? Do any of them have rules at home about this? Some families save all sweets until after tea, some limit them to once or twice a week and so on.

◆ Discuss how sugar in drinks is also harmful and we often don't realise how much sugar they contain. What sorts of drinks do the children have? Which have lots of sugar? Advise the children that water is the best drink they can have.

PSHE and citizenship activities

◆ Invite the school dentist and dental nurse or local dentist in to explain more fully what the role of a dentist and dental nurse are and the best things people can do to look after their teeth.
◆ Ask the children to make posters about how to keep teeth healthy. Use books on the topic to gain more information. Have a class competition for the best poster, with the prize of a toothbrush, for example. Display the posters and ask the headteacher or another class to judge them.

◆ In pairs, ask the children to write a set of instructions for how to brush your teeth properly. If you have not had a dentist in, use brochures from the dental surgery to inform the children about how to brush properly, and demonstrate to them how it should be done. Many of them will probably not be doing it as well as they could. Ask individuals to set goals for improving their brushing, for example brushing at night as well as in the morning, brushing for a whole minute, making sure they brush in a certain order (such as front of teeth, then back of teeth and so on), brushing up and down rather than sideways. They could keep a tick chart for a week in the bathroom to monitor their success at achieving these goals.

◆ Ask the children to keep a log of all the sweet products they eat and drink over a week. Show them some examples of hidden sugar and sweeteners in foods, for example some crisps, biscuits, white bread, squash, some juice drinks, even some breakfast cereals. Ask the children to check the lists of ingredients on the packets, tins, bottles and so on for sugar. Is it near the beginning or the end of the list? (The nearer the start, the higher its percentage.) Look at how often they consume sugary things. Do they think they could cut this down? How? Ask them to set realistic goals, for example have biscuits for a snack only every other day, keep sweets until after tea and then brush their teeth afterwards.

◆ Teach the children the names of the teeth, using a model of a mouth, if you have one, or a diagram. Ask the children to draw a plan of their mouths to show which teeth they have. Explain about wisdom teeth and how they grow later, but sometimes not at all. Have all the children got the same number of teeth? How many will they have as an adult?

◆ Discuss with the children that some teeth grow crooked and sometimes our mouths are not big enough for all our teeth so they squash up. Talk about braces and what they do, how they are fitted and so on.

◆ Introduce the subject of bacteria from food particles left in the mouth helping plaque to develop and also being passed into our stomachs. Help the children to understand that because our bodies react against them, some bacteria make us ill and therefore we need to be careful about hygiene and putting unclean things into our mouths. Ask the children to write notices to display in appropriate places in school about the importance of washing our hands before we eat and after we have been to the toilet. Let the children investigate more about this topic in textbooks.

Further literacy ideas

◆ Ask the children to write detailed descriptions about their favourite sweets or sweet food and what happens when they eat it, how they feel, what it tastes like, how it feels as they chew it, swallow it and so on.

◆ Read Michael Rosen's 'Chocolate cake' poem from *Quick, Let's Get Out of Here* (Puffin Books). Look at the style of the poem and point out that it tells a story. Ask the children to write about a similar experience, real or imagined, in a comparable style.

◆ Get the children to write a letter to the visiting dentist or dental nurse, thanking them for coming and mentioning what they learned from the visit. Look at formal letter-writing characteristics together before they start.

◆ Ask the children to remember what it was like the last time they visited the dentist and to write a diary extract recounting the experience.

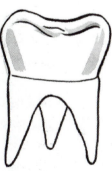

Citizenship

Citizenship within the context of Key Stage 2, revolves around five themes: management of money, including saving for the future; democracy; preserving the environment: supporting those less fortunate, including the Third World; and rules and laws.

Work on the environment and voluntary work, fund-raising for good causes and awareness of global inequalities have long been features of the primary school curriculum, forming links to geography, RE and science. Relatively new aspects to most Key Stage 2 planning frameworks are the other three:
◆ the study of democracy as a political institution, its operation and principles, at local, national and international levels
◆ the management of money, including the need to save for future need, such as for pensions
◆ the need for compliance with the laws and rules of society, together with an understanding of legitimate ways of changing laws and rules deemed to be unfair.

For teachers, these elements may require some development of existing schemes, but they are important to the children as they grow up in an increasingly complex and challenging society. The imposition of a compulsory citizenship element to the National Curriculum at Key Stages 3 and 4, as well as a voluntary one at Key Stages 1 and 2, was a response by government to concerns about the general decline in people's involvement in the democratic processes of this country and Europe. Education was deemed to be a key factor in the arresting of this decline, through the opportunities of knowledge and involvement. Enabling children to meet local MPs, MEPs and counsellors, to put their points of view to them and to attend council meetings or offices, can help support the text work given here. In addition, many schools are creating school councils to give children a democratic voice in the running of the school. This extension of the democratic principles at the immediate level can actively stimulate knowledge, commitment and understanding of the processes that govern all our lives.

Schools have always reinforced the need for compliance to the school rules, often based on common social rules, such as respecting other's property and not causing harm to others. In recent years, since the recommendations of the Elton Report (1989), many schools involve children in the formulation of class and school rules, to encourage a sense of ownership and to develop understanding of the benefits of rules. This work can be expanded to consider the country's laws, how and why they were made, what benefits they bring and, if they are considered no longer right or workable, how citizens can go about changing them without resorting to law-breaking. Together with this issue, is the need to develop a sense of collective duty to be law-abiding, even when the person doesn't agree with a law, for example cycling on the pavement, or, more controversially, the taking of illegal substances.

Finally, the desire to encourage in future adults a sense of personal responsibility towards their own financial security has led to the introduction of some work at Key Stage 2 on saving for the future. Although this can be dealt with as a short-term saving for a PlayStation game, for example, or new trainers, it nevertheless cultivates the awareness that it is not always someone else's job to provide for them. It also helps to cultivate the strength to delay gratification, a key component to managing impulses and desires. Inevitably, it contributes to the development of prudence and self-discipline and thus freedom from addictive patterns of behaviour. School saving schemes could be considered, with the involvement of banks or building societies as a practical reinforcement in addition to the work done here.

Limericks

Genre
humorous
poetry –
limericks

A brave taxi driver called Clive,

Once found a Black Mamba alive.

Though they said, "Shoot it dead!"

He decided instead

To take it round town for a drive.

A deep-water sailor called Rod

Used to dive in and rescue live cod.

He wasn't a fool

Who thought nets were cruel,

But he certainly was pretty odd.

Michael Palin

Limericks

Display information on species in danger of extinction, from the Internet and the World Wide Fund for Nature; children's own limericks and illustrations.

PSHE and citizenship learning objectives

◆ To research, discuss and debate topical issues, problems and events (2a).

◆ To accept that there are different sorts of responsibilities, rights and duties in the community (2d).

◆ To recognise the role of voluntary, community and pressure groups (2h).

◆ To appreciate that resources can be allocated in different ways and that these economic choices affect the sustainability of the environment (2j).

Background notes

These two humorous limericks can be used to introduce work on the environment especially in relation to endangered species and wildlife conservation.

Vocabulary

Extinction, limerick, wildlife, species, endangered, ecology, quotas.

Discussing the text

◆ Read the first limerick, introducing the author. Have the children heard of him already? Did they know he wrote poetry? Talk about the type of poem and ask the children how we know it is a limerick. (It has five lines with rhyming endings for lines 1, 2 and 5, and 3 and 4.) Go through the phrasing of two long lines, two short lines and one long line. Identify these features in the poem and remind the children that limericks are usually humorous.

◆ Ask the children what the limerick is about. Identify that a black mamba is a snake. Do they know if black mambas can be found in Britain in the wild? (They can't.) Why did the people want Clive to shoot it? (A black mamba is dangerous to humans.)

◆ Do the children think Clive was right not to kill the animal? Allow a range of responses, but cultivate the ideas that the snake wasn't acting in a threatening way; it has a right to exist in its own territory.

◆ Talk about how people should learn to co-exist with animals rather than destroy them. The black mamba lives deep in the jungle. Perhaps people should leave it alone. Discuss a similar example from Britain of the adder. It is a shy snake that strikes only when under attack.

◆ Ask the children why they think Michael Palin wrote this limerick. Was he trying to say something serious in a funny way? Children should justify their views.

◆ Read the second limerick. How do we know that Rod isn't saving cod because he doesn't like any cod to be hurt? (*He wasn't a fool / Who thought nets were cruel.*) Talk about these lines in this poem. Does Palin think that nets are not a cruel way to catch fish? Do the children agree? If so, why?

◆ Continue by discussing why cod are caught. Explain that fish such as cod is often part of meals like fish fingers and that fisherman go out in trawlers to catch this fish, and others, from the seas around Britain. Talk about the factory ships and the problems of over-fishing and diminishing fish stocks. Why are quotas imposed by the EC? (To prevent the extinction of the cod – it might be necessary to clarify what is meant by extinct.)

◆ Ask the children if it really matters if black mambas or cod become extinct. Play devil's advocate by suggesting that one is sometimes dangerous to humans, the other can be 'replaced' with other fish. Do they know of other animals that are under threat of extinction because of humans? (Whales, tigers, elephants, pandas, for example.)

◆ What can we do to prevent animals becoming extinct? (Protect them with international laws, regulate the stocks by quotas, not buy things using animal products from endangered species, such as ivory, give money to campaigns, speak or write to our MPs or MEPs about the matter, find out more about the animals and the dangers they are experiencing, encourage breeding programmes in captivity.)

PSHE and citizenship activities

◆ In pairs, ask the children to choose an endangered animal and to find out as much as they can about it, its habitat, diet and way of life, using the Internet and books from the library. Tell them to write a project about the animal, explaining why it is at risk and what can be done to help solve this.

◆ Invite your MEP in to talk about cod quotas and the reasons for them, including the advantages and disadvantages. If this isn't possible, the children could discuss the issues, then collectively write a letter to their MEP, asking for his or her view and any information he or she has on the matter.

◆ Contact campaign groups responsible for protecting wildlife for information about their campaigns (for example, WWF, WSPA, Friends of the Earth). In small groups, ask the children to evaluate the material, extracting a series of arguments for the preservation of species. Another group can then work on those arguments, trying to find counter-arguments. Present both sides of the debate and vote on whether the campaign deserves to be supported.

◆ Visit an RSPB or other nature reserve and learn about local animals in danger of extinction and the reasons why they are endangered (mostly destruction of habitat). The class could pledge to support a local environmental campaign by creating a wildlife area in the school grounds or by taking part in voluntary work, either under the organisation of the school or individually with parental support. They could look at helping hedgehogs, owls, frogs, wild flowers and so on.

◆ This work could be presented in an assembly on wildlife, showing the value of keeping diversity within the animal kingdom and suggesting ways of helping. The children could deliver the assembly as a press conference given by the school wildlife preservation campaign, outlining animals in danger and ways of supporting the campaign. It could include a simulated interview with a fisherman or commercial hunter putting the opposite view.

◆ Visit a local zoo or wildlife park employed in preservation and breeding programmes to learn more about the animals they are trying to protect and the work that they do.

Further literacy ideas

◆ Look at a range of limericks and identify the common characteristics of this genre and its layout. Ask the children to rework a popular tale as a limerick, for example 'Sleeping Beauty'.

◆ Ask the children to write their own limericks, based on an endangered animal of their choice.

◆ Ask the children to write a pamphlet promoting the protection of wildlife. Look at a range of similar pamphlets in the Literacy Hour to identify style and impact. Advise the children to include illustrations, bullet points and short, pithy slogans and messages.

◆ Examine formal letter characteristics and collaboratively write a letter to a wildlife organisation requesting information on endangered species and the programmes the organisation is involved in.

◆ Look at the rhyming words in the two limericks. Help the children to find other rhymes around an animal theme from which they can create a limerick. For example, *stripes – bites, horns –mourns*.

◆ Read an extract from Kipling's *The Jungle Book* and discuss the ecological views contained in it.

Fight for Blackwater

Following a class field trip to Blackwater Woods,
Class Five are in for a nasty surprise.

Genre
contemporary
fiction that
raises issues

Miss Jackson made a dramatic announcement. "You remember what a wonderful time we had at Blackwater Woods, last week, well I'm very sorry to say that I've just found out that Superprice Supermarkets now own the land. The trees will be pulled down and an enormous new megastore and car park built over it. This is terrible."

For the first time ever Class Five saw Miss Jackson struggling not to cry.

"We must stop them!" Sonja declared emphatically.

There was an echoing cheer from most of the class.

"I understand how you feel, Sonja," Miss Jackson sympathised, "but..."

"We could write to our council," Sonja rudely interrupted, her mind concentrating on the problem not her teacher's excuses.

"Or our MP!" another class member shouted out.

"The government?"

"Greenpeace?"

Carl grinned then made his own funny suggestion, "Eco-warriers?" Everyone glared at him. Carl couldn't understand it; the whole thing was daft. A supermarket was a great idea.

Miss Jackson took advantage of the momentary silence to impose some control. "You're right children. We could object. The supermarket would have to get planning permission from the council to build. Shall we write?"

Sonja wanted more direct action.

"Could we visit the council? A few of us could go and demand that our woods be saved!"

Miss Jackson wasn't certain. This wasn't what she had intended. On the other hand, she reasoned, there was a lot of educational work in this. Yes, she resolved, Class Five would lead the campaign to save Blackwater Woods.

Letters had to be written. Carl refused to take part, on principle.

"Carl," Miss Jackson suggested. "Why don't you add an entry to our website about the campaign. You might find other sites that we could use to spread news of the campaign. I think I'll put you in charge of Internet communications."

Carl blinked rapidly. He hadn't thought of that.

"Right!" he said brightly.

"Can I do it now?"

Suddenly Carl was an environmentalist.

By the end of the afternoon, Miss Jackson had four printed letters in her hands. She posted three of the four, those to the Minister for the Environment, their MP and the local branch of Greenpeace. The fourth, for the council, she would deliver in hand after school.

Suddenly the whole class was stopped dead as a series of flashes lit the classroom.

"What...? Who are you?" Miss Jackson demanded, bearing down upon the two men hovering in the open doorway.

"Press, Hislop *Courier*. About the campaign to save Blackwater Woods. Tim, get a few shots of the kids against that wall with the display."

"Er... er... How did you know?"

Carl lifted a hesitant finger. "I e-mailed them."

"Carl!" Miss Jackson exclaimed in despair. The headteacher would be furious.

"You told me to use my initiative," Carl cried in complaint.

She had indeed. The camera was snapping and Sonja was conducting her own interview with the journalist. She'd better get the official line over, and quickly before she lost her job.

Three quarters of an hour later, still accompanied by the press, Miss Jackson led the three children – Sonja, Richard and now a very proud Carl, into the imposing front entrance of the council offices. They had an appointment with the Chairman of the council. There was a chance this would work, there really was.

* * * * *

Class Five listened in absolute silence as their class teacher recounted the miserable experience at the council offices. Objections should have been raised earlier at the planning application stage. It was too late. The supermarket had permission to build.

"Never mind children," Miss added positively, "there's still hope."

"How?" Sonja asked starkly.

The teacher's cheeks and neck flamed red, her lips tightening in an effort to control her temper. "The press can be powerful. We also have yet to receive replies from the Government and our MP."

Sonja wasn't mollified.

"We have to do more!"

Miss Jackson had had enough.

"We have to do the Literacy Hour. Over to the carpet please."

Everyone recognised that tone. They scrambled to obey.

At break-time, Carl wasn't allowed to go out. He hadn't done enough work. Slumping in his chair, he mumbled quietly as he struggled to complete the questions under the eye of his teacher.

"Miss Jackson, a word."

It was the headteacher. Unaware of the boy's presence at the back of the class, she continued speaking in clipped tones.

"Whilst I encourage the children's involvement in civil affairs, I want you to stop this campaign. The school's reputation will suffer. Concentrate on raising standards, Miss Jackson and leave politics to the politicians. By the by, the regional manager of Superprice has offered four computers to the school as compensation for losing Blackwater Woods. I've accepted on your behalf and assured the man that there will be no further publicity. You do understand me?"

"Yes."

The headteacher grunted, then left, satisfied.

Carl couldn't help it, he stared at Miss Jackson. She was standing perfectly still, her face ashen.

"Out you go, Carl," she croaked.

The boy didn't wait for a second order. He was in the playground in moments.

Pulling Richard out of the football game, he babbled something about the campaign. Even more startling, Carl grabbed Sonja from her huddle of friends and dragged her, protesting, the few metres needed to secure some privacy.

"Get off, you pig! I'll thump you..."

"Shut up, Sonja and listen!"

"Carl," Richard warned.

Using strong-arm stuff with Sonja was not wise. When she wasn't saving Blackwater Woods, or the whales, she was at judo lessons.

Carl eventually got his information out. Sonja was furious. She was about to go and tell the headteacher what she thought of his low, despicable cowardice when the whistle went.

"Meet me after dinner, here!" Sonja ordered in whispered tones. A very brooding, slit-eyed girl entered the classroom after break, along with two faintly sick-looking boys.

"Right Carl, you get on that Internet and call up some help. Eco-warriors, that's what we need now," Sonja stated.

"What?!" Carl gasped, his jaw dropping in shock.

"Are you thick or something?"

"Leave it out, Sonja," Richard snapped, cross at the insult to his friend.

"You have a better idea?"

Richard ignored that, continuing, "What do you imagine e-mailing them is going to do for the campaign?"

Suddenly he understood the horror of her plan. She was going to invite the tree people to invade the woods at

Blackwater. There would be police in riot gear, bailiffs, security guards, fighting, accidents. It was terrible.

"If we can't win legally, we'll win by civil resistance."

"You're insane, Sonja," Richard snarled. "Haven't you seen them on telly? They'll do anything!"

"Exactly."

"Well, count me out," Richard spat, pivoting on his trainer heel and stomping away.

"Good riddance!" Sonja muttered. "Right, go and play with your mouse, Carl. I'm sure you can find some eco-warrior to talk to."

Carl watched wide-eyed as Sonja departed. He could just forget it, but somehow he knew he wouldn't. Why, he had no idea.

Carl waited until he was home. It was easier than he expected. Typing in 'eco-warriors' in the search box gave him several hits. It didn't take long sending messages, but not one of these was instantly replied to, they were probably up trees or down tunnels, Carl mused.

Two days later a couple letters arrived at the school for Class Five. Miss Jackson read out the contents to the class. Greenpeace was very encouraging but regretful that a shortage of funding prevented involvement. It was disappointing.

"Too busy boarding whaling ships, I suppose," Carl muttered cynically.

The next letter was even worse. It was from some civil servant in DEFRA. Miss Jackson's voice shook with emotion as she read it out. "How good to know that young children were taking an interest in their environment and learning how to use their civil rights to put forward their view, very commendable... Of course, whilst it is sad to see woodland disappear, we must look at this from the point of view of the local economy. Think how many people will get jobs building then working at the supermarket. It will reduce traffic in the town centre. Surely the loss of a few trees was worth that... The supermarket company have promised to landscape the supermarket... Keep working hard at your literacy and numeracy, children and don't worry about issues you are really too young to understand."

The air in the classroom was thick with collective anger and resentment. To be talked down to like that was insulting. Richard shot a glance in Sonja's direction. She was going to be unstoppable now.

When Carl got home that night there was an e-mail message waiting for him, "Thanks for the info but we already knew about it. We're on our way." Punching the air, Carl yelled out in triumph, then rushed downstairs. Fumbling, he telephoned Sonja. She was out at judo. Carl left a cryptic message for her, "The E-Ws are on their way."

Once the receiver was lowered Carl's sense of triumph started to fade dramatically. There would be nothing but trouble ahead, big trouble!

Gillian Goddard

Fight for Blackwater

Display a large central poster with the words *Fighting for the local environment*. From this, radiate lines with means of organising and contributing to a local campaign, for example lobbying political representatives such as MPs and councillors, working with and supporting an official pressure group such as Greenpeace, finding out about the arguments for and against the campaign and considering the merits of the case, writing to the press and television to put forward views, making a peaceful protest under parental supervision.

PSHE and citizenship learning objectives

◆ To research, discuss and debate topical issues, problems and events (2a).

◆ To know why and how rules are made and enforced and why different rules are needed in different situations (2b).

◆ To know that there are different kinds of responsibilities, rights and duties in the home, school and community and that these can sometimes conflict with each other (2d).

◆ To know what democracy is, and about the institutions that support it locally and nationally (2g).

◆ To recognise the role of voluntary, community and pressure groups (2h).

◆ To know that resources can be allocated in different ways and that these economic choices affect individuals, communities and the sustainability of the environment (2j).

◆ To explore how the media present information (2k).

◆ To value and want to preserve their local natural environment.

Background notes

This story was originally published in *Junior Focus* in June and August 1999. It looks at environmental issues, focusing particularly on ways of protesting and campaigning. The discussions could be undertaken as a linked double lesson over two days.

Vocabulary

Campaign, environmentalist, eco-warriors, media, council, planning procedures, illegal, bribery, lobby.

Discussing the text

◆ Read the first section. Check the children's comprehension by asking what the story is about and what is happening to Blackwater Woods. What did the class do at first to save their woods? Why?

◆ Carl is not an environmentalist. How do we know what his views are about Blackwater Woods? Ask the children to point out the sentences that tell us. Is his view valid? (Yes, he is entitled to favour the presence of a supermarket over a wood.) On a flip chart, list all possible arguments for saving the woods on one side and on the other, all possible arguments for wanting a supermarket. Ask the children to vote on which side they would have belonged in the story.

◆ Ask the children why Carl eventually becomes involved in the campaign. (He is given a chance to use the Internet, which he enjoys.) Was his commitment to the aims of the campaign strong? Make the point that sometimes people join campaigns for reasons other than genuine interest or commitment to the cause. Ask children to think of some reasons why people might do this. (For example, to be with their friends, to feel included, to get out of doing something less pleasant, to feel powerful, even to cause trouble.)

◆ What do the children think about Sonja? Was she popular and if not, why not? Why do activists sometimes make us feel uncomfortable? (They make us feel guilty.) Are activists valuable though?

◆ What did Carl do that upset Miss Jackson? Why was Miss Jackson so unhappy about the press reporting the class campaign? Was she right? Do the press sometimes make things worse?

◆ Read on and check that the children have understood what has happened. Ask why the council and Department of Environment failed to support the class's campaign. Were these bodies right, do the children think?

◆ Why did the headteacher order Miss Jackson to stop the campaign? Was the headteacher right to accept the computers or was it bribery? List the points for and against.

◆ Ask the children to recall what Sonja decided was going to be the next move in the campaign. What are eco-warriors and what do they do? Introduce the idea of civil disobedience. Discuss whether this is a legitimate form of protest. Make sure children understand that illegal action is wrong. Protesting must always be carried out in a legal way.

◆ What is likely to be the outcome? Why is Carl so worried? In pairs, ask the children to discuss the question *Will Blackwater Woods be saved?* (The concluding section was published in *Junior Focus* in September 1999.)

P SHE and citizenship activities

◆ Find out about local areas of publicly held land. Map these out, one group taking responsibility for each site, then ask each group to put forward arguments for the retention of these pieces of land in their current form.

◆ Together, write to or e-mail Greenpeace to find out more about their work.

◆ Take the children on a visit to the local council offices to look at the work of the planning committee, or invite a planning officer or committee member to talk about the issues they consider when approving planning applications.

◆ As a class, compose a letter to the local MP asking for the government's policy on urban development in respect of environmental issues. Alternatively, you could access this information through the DEFRA website (www.defra.gov.uk).

◆ Ask the children to consult with the adults in their families about their views on eco-warriors and their actions. Tell them to bring that information back for a class discussion on the methods employed by eco-warriors and the reasons for their popularity or unpopularity.

◆ Discuss possible conclusions to the story, then, in small groups, ask the children to choose their favourite ending and act it out for the class.

Further literacy ideas

◆ Conduct a formal class debate on the merits of saving Blackwater Woods or building a supermarket. Organise the children to role-play Superprice managers on one side, Sonja and Greenpeace on the other, with the local MP in the position of chairperson.

◆ Ask the children to imagine they are Sonja and write an ordered plan of action to save Blackwater Woods. Tell them to make a list of the things to do in terms of priority and time and that they should be summarising and writing in succinct points.

◆ Using the computer, help the children to create a newspaper report about the class campaign to save Blackwater Woods. Encourage them to include pictures and the interviews with Sonja and Miss Jackson.

◆ In small groups, ask the children to adapt the first section of the story into playscript format.

The Countryside Code

Genre
instructions –
a series of
public notices
and signs

Keep off the grass

Put your litter in the bins provided

Don't bathe in the pond

Keep to the paths through the wood

Don't feed the wild animals

Don't light fires

Shut the gates

The Countryside Code

Display a large representation, with illustrations, of the Countryside Code (from libraries or from the Countryside Agency at www.countryside.gov.uk).

PSHE and citizenship learning objectives

◆ To research, discuss and debate topical issues, problems and events (2a).

◆ To know why and how rules and laws are enforced, and why different rules are needed for different situations (2b).

◆ To understand the consequences of anti-social behaviour on individuals and communities (2c).

◆ To recognise that pressure to behave in an unacceptable or risky way can come from a variety of sources, including the people they know (3f).

Vocabulary

Rules, signs, code, enforceable, deterrent, sanctions, environment, peer pressure.

Discussing the text

◆ Read the signs. Ask the children what they are and where they might be seen. What are they for? (They are instructions or warnings.) Examine the way they are presented – in simple, straightforward language, in short sentences, with diagrams. Can the children recall any other similar signs around the school or local area?

◆ What is the overall purpose of these signs? (To preserve the environment and wildlife, to keep people safe, to avoid spoiling the place.)

◆ Ask: *What would happen to you if you disobeyed these rules?* Explain that, sometimes, the rules are enforceable by law and have penalties for breaking them, such as fines for dropping litter. Discuss with the children whether it is fair to have such enforceable rules about the park or streets or in school, where you might get into trouble if you break the rules. (Explore the idea of a deterrent and a sanction to make it clear that the rule is an important one for the good of everyone.)

◆ Talk about the reasons why some people break these rules or do not follow the instructions. (They just don't want to, or want to do the opposite, they don't care about the reasons the rules have been made, they don't think they will be caught, they don't value the environment, their friends make them.) Go on to talk about what would happen if everyone behaved or thought like this.

◆ Ask the children if there is any other way, other than sanctions, for encouraging prevention of damage to the environment. (Perhaps education and peer pressure.)

PSHE and citizenship activities

◆ Look around the classroom and playground and find any instructional signs. Ask the children in small groups to identify the reasons for their presence and assess whether or not the demands made by them are reasonable.

◆ In pairs, ask the children to create new signs designed to help maintain the pleasant environment of the playground, school and class. They could include text such as *Don't drop litter, Keep your desk tidy, Put your chairs in when you leave your desk.*

◆ Look at some rule books or lists of rules, such as the Countryside Code, the Green Cross Code, fire drill procedure and your school rules. In pairs, ask the children to choose one rule from one of the lists and prepare a brief presentation to an infant group, explaining why the rule is there and what it means for us.

◆ Ask the children to write a story about a group of friends who go into the park and drop litter, chase the ducks, climb the trees and play about on the little children's play equipment. Tell the children: *You are one of the friends and you are telling the story in the first person. What happens when you try to stop your friends being silly and breaking the rules?*

◆ In groups, help the children to plan a nature park. Advise them to present a large-scale plan, with an assessment of how the planing group will ensure that the place is not spoiled. What signs will they need? What sanctions will be imposed for breaching those rules?

◆ Ask the children to find out what the local council's by-laws are by writing to the local council. Discuss who the laws are aimed at. Who or what do they help? Do they help to prevent accidents, traffic congestion, disputes and so on?

Further literacy ideas

◆ Ask the children to write a procedural list of rules for keeping their bedrooms clean and tidy.

◆ Ask the children to use the word processor to design a sign with one of the rules you have been talking about. Remind them to make sure that the layout is attractive and the message easily understood, that the text is large and the language is simple and in short sentences.

◆ Look at the difference between instructions and requests. Emphasise that one is *telling* and one is *asking*. Get the children to translate the school rules or class rules into requests. For example, *Keep the classroom tidy – Could you please keep the classroom tidy? Don't speak when someone else is speaking – Do you think you could wait until someone has finished speaking before you speak?*

Defining democracy

Democracy (n) A form of political government that requires and allows all members of a state or country to have an equal right to participate in the government of that state, either through direct say or by electing a representative. (f. Fr *démocratie* via Gk *demokratia* [*demos* – 'the people', *kratia* – 'power or strength'])

Demobili...
to disb...
t... out of mobil-
...from the
...pa.p.
...the

Democrat, one who adheres to or promotes democracy as a princip... member of the Democrat in the ...tted States, the party generali... ghts of States against centralisat... a low tariff... in several seat... democratic... being ... to ...

BALLOT PAPER

Defining democracy

Make a presentation of UK national democratic institutions and figures (for example, Prime Minister, English Parliament – the Houses of Commons and Lords; Scottish Parliament and Welsh and Irish Assemblies; MPs, MSPs, MLAs, AMs) connected to a voting ballot box with a voter casting a vote.

PSHE and citizenship learning objectives

◆ To research, discuss and debate topical issues, problems and events (2a).

◆ To know how laws are made and enforced (2b).

◆ To know that there are different kinds of responsibilities, at home, at school and in the community (2d).

◆ to know what democracy is, and about the basic institutions that support it locally and nationally (2g).

Background notes

Year 5 and 6 children may well find these political discussions more interesting than younger children do. This work could combine well with studying Ancient Greece in history.

Vocabulary

Democracy, vote, school council, representative, elect, parliament, Assembly, government, referendum.

Discussing the text

◆ Start by putting the word *democracy* on a board or flip chart and asking the children what it means. They might say something like *a country where people vote for their government* or *a country where people are free.* Then display and read the text and establish that it is a dictionary definition. Show an example of a children's dictionary and ask someone to find the word *democracy* and read out the definition. Record this on the board alongside the photocopied text to help the children understand the meanings.

◆ Using a highlighter pen, together identify in the first text the key words that help us to understand what democracy is: *government that requires and allows all members… to have an equal right to participate.* Ask the children what that means in practice. Confirm that they understand that in Britain's democracy all people aged 18 and over have an equal right to vote for Parliament or Assembly Members who may then be selected from parliament to form the government, and the right extends to their being represented by an MP, MSP, AM or MLA in parliament.

◆ Ask the children if they know what parliament does. (It passes laws that have to be obeyed by all the people.) Why do we have a parliament? Why don't we just elect a party leader to run the country without a parliament? (There is a need for all sorts of views to be represented. Emphasise to the children that the text refers to *all* members. Important choices should be made through discussion and debate rather than one person deciding everything. Make links to freedom of speech.)

◆ Relate the parliamentary functions to those of the school council (if you have one). What do they have in common? What is different? (Usually the school council cannot make school rules or change them without the agreement of the headteacher and governors, but they do provide a voice and a collective, popular view.)

◆ Look at the part of the text that identifies democracy as being *representative* or *direct*. Explain the difference using the example of a referendum when everyone can vote on an issue directly (use a school or class example if preferred) and when we vote for MPs to represent our views and vote for us. Why do we have representatives, rather than every one of us sitting in parliament and voting for laws? (It's not practical, it would take too long and be very expensive.)

PSHE and citizenship activities

◆ In groups, using information books and CD-ROMs and the Internet (for example www.parliament.uk), ask the children to find out about our government – the political parties, Parliaments and Assemblies and their members. Ask them to produce a poster, with clear explanations and illustrations. These should then form part of the display.

◆ Talk with children about other political and governmental systems such as fascism, military dictatorship, oligarchy, monarchy, communism. Explain clearly what the features are. In groups, ask the children to identify the advantages and disadvantages of these systems and compare them with our democracy.

◆ As a whole class, identify countries that the children think have a democratic system of government.

◆ Arrange a visit to the local council offices. Look at the electoral register and have a talk about when elections take place locally and nationally. Look at the council chamber and, if possible, stay for a small part of a council meeting.

◆ Ask the children to write their own definitions of democracy and democratic, for younger children to understand.

◆ Invite a local MP or prospective parliamentary candidate to come in and talk about the process of an election, the role of MPs and why it is so important to vote.

Further literacy ideas

◆ Look at the layout of a dictionary. Let the children use dictionaries and thesauruses to find words to do with government and democracy, for example *parliament*, *vote*, *council*, *representative*, *ballot*. Tell them to write sentences using these words.

◆ Explore the derivation of the word *democracy*. Explain that it comes from two Ancient Greek words: *demos* (people) and *kratia* (power or strength). Help the children to appreciate that *people power* or *people strength* is what democracy basically means. More able children might know or be able to find other *demos* words, such as *demagogue* and *demograph*. Ask all the children to find the derivations of other long words by looking at dictionaries. They could look at, for example, words ending in *graphy* or *metry*, or beginning *geo* or *bi*. Tell them to work out how they were formed and to write etymological explanations of their favourite words.

◆ Ask the children to draw and caption a line diagram illustrating the process of voting for MPs and representation in parliament.

◆ Ask the children to design and write a leaflet aiming to persuade people to exercise their democratic rights by voting.

Emmeline Pankhurst

Genre
*historical
biography*

Mrs Pankhurst was born in the middle of the Victorian period, in 1858. At that time, most men and all women were unable to vote in general elections. They were disenfranchised. Emmeline Pankhurst became a champion for the voting rights of women, for 'women's suffrage' as it was called. Women who actively supported her campaign were called suffragettes. In 1889, she founded the Women's Franchise League, which succeeded in getting married women the right to vote in local elections in 1894. Single women were still unable to vote.

Mrs Pankhurst held public office at local government level for several years, then in 1903, she founded the Woman's Social and Political Union (WSPU). The union's campaigns achieved widespread publicity because the women supporting them were noisy and troublesome and eventually moved into violent action against property – smashing windows and on one occasion burning a hole in a golf club's greens. They did not attack people however, though several suffragettes lost their lives for the cause.

Suffragettes spoke out at other political party meetings, often getting thrown out of the halls. They marched down streets, singing their campaign songs and sporting the union's colours of green and yellow on sashes. They held demonstrations, including chaining themselves to railings to prevent the police from carrying them away. The women were often hurt when they were arrested and were frequently fined and imprisoned.

Many women, including Mrs Pankhurst and her daughters Christabel and Sylvia, suffered greatly for their involvement in this organisation. It was a very active, public campaign that received a massive amount of publicity and condemnation from men and women who felt that women were incapable of voting sensibly because they had weak brains and were too emotional.

In 1908–9 Mrs Pankhurst was imprisoned three times. By 1912, suffragettes in prison were routinely going on hunger strike to protest at their imprisonment. They were force-fed in very cruel ways. This produced a reaction from the public who felt the actions of prison staff were wrong. The Liberal Government was forced to reconsider its

policy, but contrived a clever act known as the 'Cat and Mouse Act' (1913) which permitted women prisoners to be released for short periods when their health had worsened through starvation. The women were re-arrested and imprisoned after a few weeks and often repeated the hunger-striking action. Mrs Pankhurst herself, was released and re-imprisoned a dozen times in one year, serving a total of 30 days in prison.

When the First World War broke out, the campaign was suspended and Mrs Pankhurst put her full political efforts into supporting the war effort. So many men were killed in that war that women were, of necessity, allowed to work in previously male-only occupations. People who had opposed female suffrage, saw that women could be productive, intelligent, sensible and strong, taking on tough jobs without harm. Women experienced the freedoms that come from being able to earn a living without needing a man to support them financially.

When the war ended, Mrs Pankhurst was 60 years of age. Her daughter Christabel ran the suffrage campaign whilst Mrs Pankhurst travelled extensively abroad, lecturing on the need for women to get jobs and contribute to the economy. She returned to England in 1926, at the age of 68, and immediately stood as a candidate for parliament. She died in 1928, the very year that women achieved the same voting rights as men by the passing of the Representation of the People Act.

Mrs Pankhurst was frequently demonised in the press. She was a difficult woman who could be very hard on her fellow campaigners. She was, however, a very brave and intelligent campaigner, who refused to be cowed or deterred by the male political establishment who, for the most part, were absolutely determined not to let women vote. The efforts she and her fellow suffragettes made, need to be remembered and applauded. It was largely due to her campaign, followed by women proving their worth during the war, that women in this country have the freedom today to take part in political processes, as voters, councillors and MPs.

Emmeline Pankhurst

Display illustrated investigative pieces of the children's writing on Mrs Pankhurst and the female suffrage campaign.

PSHE and citizenship learning objectives

◆ To research, discuss and debate topical issues, problems and events (2a).

◆ To recognise how and why laws are made and enforced and how to take part in making and changing laws (2b).

◆ To understand that there are different types of responsibilities, rights and duties, at home, at school and in the community (2d).

◆ To know what democracy is and about the basic institutions that support it locally and nationally (2g).

◆ To recognise the role of pressure groups (2h).

◆ To explore how the media present information (2k).

◆ To understand the importance of taking part in democratic activities.

◆ To consider appropriate and legal ways of bringing about political change.

Background notes

This text looks at democracy through the story of Emmeline Pankhurst and her fight for getting women the right to vote. The fight was extremely long and difficult. Many women and some men suffered personally and painfully to achieve a basic human right of equality and to achieve real democracy. The struggle women went through deserves greater study, perhaps as part of the Victorians history study unit, though realisation came later. If possible, recreate a climate of inequality in petty ways against the girls first, then the boys, in a simulation to help the children identify with such injustice. Make sure the children consent to this and understand its purpose before undertaking in it.

Vocabulary

Vote, suffrage, suffragettes, hunger strike, campaign, democratic rights, protest.

Discussing the text

◆ Read the text with the children. Ask them what sort of writing it is. (A biography of an important famous person.) What did Mrs Pankhurst do that made her famous?

◆ How important was it that women should get the right to vote for local councillors and for MPs and MEPs? Encourage a range of views. Many may think it isn't important. Ask them why. Talk about the importance of *all* people being able to take part in elections for the government of the country. Emphasise that by its very nature, democracy works best when all people take part.

◆ Ask the children to find details in the text about the sorts of things the suffragettes did as part of their campaign. List these on a board or flip chart. Which of the campaign tactics do the children agree with? Ask them to discuss this in pairs and be ready to feed back to the class with reasons for any aspects of the campaign they disapprove of. Record these feelings and reasons in brief against the list, with ticks for approval and crosses for disapproval. Go on to discuss other ways campaigns for political change could or should be conducted. (For example, publicising through the press, pamphlets and the Internet; holding meetings; lobbying MPs; holding peaceful marches or demonstrations.)

◆ Ask the children why they think the suffragettes resorted to attacks on property. (To get attention and to vicariously hurt the people who were opposing them. It helped them not to be dismissed as petty and unimportant.)

◆ How do we know that the suffragettes were deeply serious about getting the freedom to vote? (They were prepared to suffer verbal and physical hurt, to be imprisoned and to risk their own lives.)

◆ Ask the children what they think Mrs Pankhurst would have been like to work for. Which parts of the text tell us a little about her personality?

◆ If Mrs Pankhurst came back today would she be pleased with what she saw? Talk about the fact that women are MPs (even PM), councillors and so on (as well as being able to vote) and many are powerful figures in business. What might Mrs Pankhurst be unhappy about? (Unequal pay rates that still exist, women being under-represented in Parliament and the Cabinet.) Make the point that she might, however, consider that women are neglecting their family roles in favour of professional ones.

P SHE and citizenship activities

◆ In pairs, let the children find out more about the campaigns for either female or male suffrage in the UK, from information books, the Internet and history or encyclopaedia CD-ROMs. Ask them to write summaries with illustrations for the wall display.

◆ Pretend that men and women do not have the vote yet. In small groups, ask the children to elect a suffrage leader and write a speech for the leader to deliver, explaining why people should be given the vote and urging the crowd to support them in their campaign.

◆ In these suffrage campaign groups, ask the children to work out a plan for the campaign. How would they run it in the present day? What media would they use to promote their message? What would they do and avoid doing to further their cause? Ask the groups to present their campaign plans to the class and answer questions posed by the 'audience'.

◆ Invite a female MP or councillor to talk about their role and why they think it is important that everyone is allowed to get involved in the political processes of democracy.

◆ Ask the children to put themselves in the place of a suffragette in prison who is refusing food. Tell them to write a diary about their feelings and the reasons why they are taking that course of action. Remind the children that they were protesting about their wrongful imprisonment and ill-treatment as well as their lack of voting rights.

◆ In small groups, ask the children to choose a scene from the biography to illustrate Mrs Pankhurst's campaign and enact this scene to the rest of the groups.

Further literacy ideas

◆ Look at other biographies of significant people and together identify the key characteristics of a biographical text, such as the recount style usually in chronological order, dates of birth and death, key achievements and their impact on society, some comments on the personality and motivations of the person.

◆ Ask the children to look for information about other famous politicians and campaigners and write a brief biography giving details of the person's life and achievements. Combine these to make a book of famous political figures.

◆ Look at the use of the suffix -ette in the word suffragette. What does it denote and on what other occasions is it used? Let the children find other -ette words using a dictionary, for example soubrette, serviette, pipette, then write sentences explaining the meaning of the word.

◆ Ask the children to word-process a campaign leaflet using persuasive language. These could be used to introduce the next text.

Hannah Gigglesworthy

– Fun For All

Vote for Hannah Gigglesworthy
Your Fun For All Party Candidate

Ms Gigglesworthy is a fine upstanding citizen who has been an active member of the Fun For All Party for five years. She is worthy of your vote and will represent your views and bring fun to all of you.

Giles Harpenden, Party Leader

A personal message from Hannah

Friends and Voters, you know me and you know what I stand for. Trust me to represent you in parliament. Vote for me on Election Day. Together, I promise we can bring this miserable government down and replace it with a fun-filled and party-loving group of MPs who will ensure that our manifesto is fulfilled in law.

As soon as we are elected as your government we will bring in laws to make sure that

- you don't have to go to work when you don't want to
- you can party all night
- you laugh at least four times a day
- you can celebrate anything you like in the street.

(Manifesto clauses 2, 4, 6, 8b)

Do you want fun?
Do you want a good time?
If so, vote for me and let's party
together on election night.

Vote Gigglesworthy. Vote for Fun

If you would like to join the Fun For All Party or donate money to the party funds, telephone 01149 1492385 for details or visit our website at www.funforallparty.co.uk.

Hannah Gigglesworthy – Fun For All

Display the children's campaign leaflets, with a point by point description of the key features of a persuasive campaign leaflet.

PSHE and citizenship learning objectives

◆ To know what democracy is and about the basic institutions that support it locally and nationally (2g).

◆ To explore how the media and specific campaigners present information (2k).

◆ To identify persuasive techniques in writing that attempt to influence voting patterns.

◆ To make reasoned choices about who to vote for and why.

Vocabulary

Candidate, party, vote, election, bias, persuasive language, omissions, information, manifesto, pledge.

Discussing the text

◆ Ask the children what this text is and what is its purpose. Identify specialised words, for example *party*, *vote*, *candidate* and *manifesto*, and ensure that the children know what each of these words mean. Record the words and their definitions given by the children on a board or flip chart.

◆ Ask the children if they have seen similar leaflets at home, or posters in windows or in the street. Show some examples if possible. (These are usually available from local political party offices. Make sure you have them from a range of parties, not just one.) Why do political parties send out these leaflets? Who are they for? What are they trying to do?

◆ Look at the text with the children and identify sections that give information and those that are trying to persuade the reader to vote for the candidate. Itemise the information on the board, for example *an active member of the Fun For All Party for five years*. Do the same for words or phrases that are persuasive in intention, for example *She is worthy of your vote*, *Trust me to represent you*.

◆ Ask the children to think about what this party is offering. Would they vote for this candidate? Ask the children to justify their answer either way. Together, work through in detail what is good about these manifesto ideas and what is bad. Are they practical? Has the leaflet highlighted important local and national issues that the candidate and party will address?
Has anyone has changed their views?

◆ Ask the children if there is anything missing from this leaflet. Is there some other information a voter would want to know before making his or her decision? (For example, all the manifesto pledges, not just a selection.) Would they like to meet Ms Gigglesworthy first and talk to her before they vote for her? Why? (The leaflet is too biased and gives only a simplistic view.)

PSHE and citizenship activities

◆ In small groups, ask the children to formulate a specific party manifesto and from it a name for the party, for example the Free Crisps For All Party, the Freedom From School Party, the Children in Government Party. Ask the groups to present their manifesto pledges to the class.

◆ Ask the children to design a leaflet using the text as an example, or to edit and polish any they word-processed earlier. Advise them that they should be trying to persuade their classmates to vote for them and their party. Suggest that they include a little bit of background about themselves and brief information on what they intend to do if they get elected to parliament. Encourage them to use various desktop publishing programmes and tools to make the leaflet eye-catching and appealing.

◆ Hold an election, with one candidate per group. Hold a secret ballot, mimicking the electoral process with a class electoral roll, a ballot box, voting slips (to be marked by Xs, not ticks), instructions for how to vote in booths, and electoral officers registering who has voted. Before voting, go through each stage of the process with the children, explaining how it works and what it is for. (For example, to make it as easy as possible for everyone to vote, to ensure everyone's vote is valid, to avoid any ballot-rigging or cheating.) Hold a count and announce the results, giving the speeches.

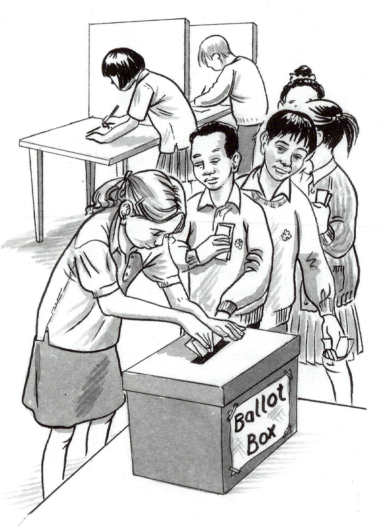

Further literacy ideas

◆ Ask the children to imagine themselves as journalists following Ms Gigglesworthy on her campaign trail. Tell them to write a newspaper account of the campaign. Advise them to include a description of Ms Gigglesworthy and her promises, the people she meets and the meetings she attends. Explain that you want them to write it from a specific point of view: either disliking Ms Giggleworthy and her party or as a supporter of them, and use the different versions to demonstrate bias in media reporting.

◆ If you held class elections (see the PSHE and citizenship activities above), ask the children to write a newspaper article describing the class election results. Advise them to consider the style of language used in reporting serious news events and that information needs to be delivered succinctly, with some political comment made on the significance of the outcome. They should also include an attractive, exciting headline.

◆ Ask the children to write a manual for political candidates, telling them how to make their leaflets persuasive. They could write under headings such as *How to make the message attractive, How to make the punter send money or join, How to summarise in bullet points, How to avoid offence, How to write slogans.*

◆ Look at a range of other persuasive material from politics, sales bumph, advertisements and so on. Ask the children to identify what is the most effective from these in influencing the reader. Remind them to include reference to layout, size of typeface and use of colour.

◆ Starting from the words and definitions you noted on the board, make a political wordbank with the class. Encourage the children to write clear definitions, for example *campaign* – an organised course of action to encourage public interest, especially before an election.

Scribbleboy

Genre
contemporary
fiction by a
significant
author (in
informal
letter format)

Scribbletation*S*, New Kid

Welcome to the neighbourhood!
    Don't know your name yet (that'*S* why I've addre*SS*ed the envelope to 'The New Kid Around Here') ...but let me introduce my*S*elf.
    My name i*S* Ziggy Fuzz.
    I'm the Pre*S*ident of a very *S*pecial fan club.
    And I'd like you – ye*S*, you, New Kid Around Here! – to join.
    The full title of the fan club i*S* the *S*cribbleboy Fan Club.
    Now, a*S* you're a New Kid Around Here, you're probably wondering who *S*cribbleboy i*S*.
    *S*o let me explain!
    If you look around the neighbourhood you'll *S*ee lot*S* of graffiti. Mo*S*t of it i*S* totally ugly and boring. But there are *S*ome piece*S* of graffiti that are not totally ugly and boring at all. That'*S* becau*S*e ...they're not graffiti!
    They're *S*cribble*S*!
    *S*cribble*S* *S*cribbled by the   mo*S*t *S*cribbledaciou*S* and *S*cribblefabulou*S* *S*cribbler in *S*cribbledom.
    Hi*S* name?
    *S*CRIBBLEBOY!!!
    You're very lucky, New Kid Around Here, becau*S*e there happen*S* to be a *S*cribble very clo*S*e to you. If you want to *S*ee it (and I'm *S*ure after reading thi*S* you'll be ru*S*hing to get an eyeful), then leave your flat*S*, cro*SS* the *S*quare, and walk down the concrete path until you reach the playground.
    At the back of thi*S* playground i*S* ...
    A *S*CRIBBLE!
    Before you go, though, a word of warning: don't mention *S*cribbleboy to grown-up*S*! I've noticed you live with your Dad and older brother – and I'm *S*ure they're very nice – but, a*S* grown-up*S*, they will not be capable of appreciating the full *S*cribblewonderment of *S*cribbleboy.
    If, when you *S*ee the *S*cribble, it *S*wirl*S* and whirl*S* in*S*ide you (like it *S*wirl*S* and whirl*S* in*S*ide me) then...
    JOIN THE *S*CRIBBLEBOY FAN CLUB!!!
    There are hundred*S* of u*S*!
    If not thou*S*and*S*!
    We meet every Tue*S*day afternoon at 5.30pm in the old cinema down the Big Road (ju*S*t walk to the back of your flat*S* and turn left into the Big Road – the old cinema i*S* on the right).
    I look forward to *S*eeing you there, New Kid Around Here.

*S*cribbleboy For Ever

Ziggy Fuzz

Pre*S*ident of the *S*cribbleboy Fan Club

P*S* If thi*S* letter i*S* opened by mi*S*take – either by the New Kid Around Here'*S* dad or the New Kid Around Here'*S* brother – then it *S*houldn't have been, a*S* I clearly marked the envelope, 'TO THE NEW KID AROUND HERE. VERY PRIVATE AND PER*S*ONAL. NOT TO BE OPENED BY ANY GROWN-UP*S*!'

PP*S* The letter '*S*' on my typewriter don't work!

Philip Ridley

Scribbleboy

Make a two-sided display, one with attractive murals designed by children and the other with examples of ugly graffiti on walls and doors. Add a maxim along the lines of *It's OK to create dazzling murals with the permission of the owner or community. It's NOT OK to deface public property with graffiti because it spoils the environment.*

PSHE and citizenship learning objectives

◆ To research, discuss and debate topical issues, problems and events (2a).

◆ To know why and how rules and laws are made and enforced. (2b)

◆ To realise the consequences of anti-social behaviours on individuals and communities (2c).

Background notes

This extract introduces the theme of abiding by laws and rules. It focuses on graffiti and its related activity of vandalism. *Scribbleboy* allows children to explore the morality of these acts, yet avoids making simple judgements.

Vocabulary

Mural, graffiti, scribble, deface, illegal, damage, fan club.

Discussing the text

◆ Read the text with the children. Make sure that they understand that this is the opening chapter in the book *Scribbleboy* by Philip Ridley. Ask them what this chapter tells us about the story.

◆ Discuss the children's ideas for what might happen next. They may raise safety and child protection issues. Discuss these and affirm good safety rules such as it not being a good idea to go alone to the old cinema and the reader should tell an adult about the letter, despite advice from the writer not to. If these views don't come up, ask the children whether or not they would go to the old cinema, and build safety talk into this discussion.

◆ Ask the children if they have seen any examples of graffiti in school or around the streets or their homes. How do they feel about that graffiti? Would they rather it wasn't there?

◆ Write *scribbles* and *graffiti* on a board or flip chart. Ask the children to explain the difference between these two as given by Ziggy. Record these distinctions under the headings. Discuss with the children whether or not they consider some graffiti to be OK: beautiful, artistic, clever. Why?

◆ Tell the children that leaving graffiti is illegal. Ask the question *Why is it illegal?* (It damages and defaces private and public property.) Do the children think leaving graffiti is wrong? Why or why not? Compare someone scrawling graffiti on the children's houses to someone scribbling on their pencil cases or books. How would they feel about that?

◆ Talk about the way many adults view graffiti. Discuss the kinds of negative messages it gives about the people in the community or school. Refer the children to the way Ziggy stresses the importance of not telling grown-ups about what's going on.

◆ Explain that there is a legal way of creating beautiful 'scribbles' on walls. These are called murals and permission will have been given for a wall or surface to be decorated with artwork, to make it look more attractive. Have the children seen any around? Is there somewhere in school or in the community that they think would be enhanced with a mural?

◆ Ziggy runs a fan club for Scribbleboy. Ask the children what a fan club is and who and what it is for? How do the children think Scribbleboy feels about having a fan club? Is it likely to encourage him to carry on? (Yes.)

PSHE and citizenship activities

◆ Ask the children to write the next chapter in the story, from the point of view of the *New Kid Around Here*. Encourage the children to explore the consequences of this child's actions.

◆ What would Ziggy do if Scribbleboy was arrested for defacing public property? Ask the children in groups to make up a role-play, acting as the fan club members. What range of action is available? (For example, asking parents to support, writing to the council to explain that no harm was intended, contacting the press to present their position, supporting Scribbleboy in court.)

◆ In pairs, ask the children to decide on an area of the classroom, school or community space that would benefit from a mural and let them design a mural for this space. Tell them to identify the colours to be used and the reasons for any themes or images they select. For example, toys and animals for the nursery play area wall, perhaps a countryside theme for an urban concrete shopping centre to make it more pleasant.

◆ As a class, choose a design for the classroom display and collaboratively create the artwork by allocating segments to each pair or individual children.

◆ Go out on a field walk and take photographs of graffiti. Discuss whether the graffiti spoils the area or not. Use the photographs and the children's own examples to create a display. The children should then generate slogans to discourage graffiti writing.

◆ Ask someone from the rail company (if there tends to be a lot of graffiti on its property) or the police to come in and talk about the problems they have with graffiti, the difficulty and expense of removing it and so on, and what happens to those who are caught vandalising in this way.

Further literacy ideas

◆ Look at the text for its use of the exclamation mark. Why are exclamation marks used? Why has this author used so many? Ask the children to write some sentences using exclamation marks appropriately.

◆ Examine the text for nonsense words, such as *scribbledacious*. How has the author created nonsense words? (By combining or adapting real words.) Why has he done it? (It's fun to make up phonetic words and there isn't an existing word that adequately expresses the feeling or action.) Do the children think this works well in the text? Encourage them to create their own nonsense words by combining two words, and then construct suitable sentences to contain them.

◆ Look at different forms of letter writing style. What sort is this? (Informal, chatty, to a potential friend, someone of a similar age.) Together, find some examples in the text that prove this is a letter (such as the salutation and signature). Ask the children to translate this letter into a formal letter of invitation.

◆ Remind the children that this text is the opening chapter in *Scribbleboy*. Would they like to read more or not? In groups, ask the children to share their views and record the reasons why some members thinks that the book is worth going on with and others feel it isn't worth reading further.

◆ Ridley uses unconventional sentences in this letter. In pairs, ask the children to find some examples of technically incorrect sentences, such as *His name?* and *If not thousands!* and translate them into correct sentences. Would the correct sentences work better in the text, or does Ridley's unconventional style add something to the character and flow of the piece? Tell the children to share their views with their work partner.

Set a thief to catch a thief

Jez is lying in bed in hospital. His mum and sister Suzanna have come to visit him. Suzanna has taken a fistful of Jez's chocolates.

Genre
contemporary fiction that raises issues, serial story

"Suzanna," their mother said patiently, "taking things without asking is wrong. It's stealing. Put them back, then Jeremy will let you have some."

Suzanna smiled sweetly and returned half of the chocolates, the other half neatly concealed in the fold of her skirt. Mother didn't see. She never did, thought Jez resentfully.

"I've some good news," his mother said. "The doctor says you can come home tomorrow, but you must stay quiet for a while until that rib is properly healed."

Jez had hurt himself in a fall. In the process, he'd nearly been electrocuted on railway lines and was lucky to be alive. He still hadn't got over the shock of it all.

"You can play with Suzanna, Jeremy. It will do you good!"

Jez wondered if his mother was making some terrible joke. He hoped so, for the prospect of being trapped indoors with his annoying little sister scared him rigid.

Four days later, Jez was beginning to think he'd go stark raving mad being stuck indoors. His mum was getting lunch.

"Oh damn! Not enough bread.

I'll pop out to the petrol station. I won't be long," she concluded.

"I'll do it," Jez offered, eagerly.

The woman smiled. "That's very kind Jeremy but I don't think…"

The insistent ring of the telephone interrupted her. Jez saw his chance. He gave his mother an appealing look, the best he could manage, and was rewarded with a weary nod. Grabbing his mum's purse, he dashed out of the house with a cheery wave.

Jez couldn't believe how much he was enjoying being outside. Whistling as he sauntered along, he failed to notice a small figure dogging his steps, a pace or two behind.

"Where are you going?" Suzanna asked with a sly smile.

"Nowhere, you toad! Go home. Mum will kill you for coming out without asking!"

"No she won't. I'm with you," Suzanna replied cockily.

Jez's chest was hurting too much to risk a push or punch, anyway the lights were changing. Praying that none of his friends would see him, he took hold of his sister's hand and saw her safely across the road.

They were still hand in hand when they walked into the petrol station shop. It was empty except for two youths going up to the counter. Suzanna skipped off to the sweet section, whilst Jez scanned the bread shelf.

Suddenly the boy felt the hairs on the back of his neck stand up.

Something was wrong. It was the expression on the face of the woman behind the counter. She was terrified. The second of the two youths turned abruptly, a baseball bat held menacingly in his hands.

"Get over there, now!" he yelled.

Yanking Suzanna hard, Jez shoved her into the corner then stood directly in front of her to protect her.

"Get off, Jez! I can't see!" the girl cried.

Jez ignored her, his body pressed close against her to keep her safe.

All the while his eyes never left the wildly swinging bat that was being brandished about, the youth laughing as he smashed up the displays for the sheer hell of it. His fellow thief was threatening the shop assistant. In blind terror, she thrust fistfuls of cash into a cloth bag.

All of a sudden, alarm bells began to ring loudly. It caused the two robbers to jump in shock. They started to fight amongst themselves. One wanted to stay and have all the cash; the other wanted to scarper. A police siren ended the dispute. The two youths visibly jerked at the sound, then made for the door.

Simultaneously Jez found himself elbowed aside. There was a flash of red dress in front of him as Suzanna ran away in panic. He had no time to call out before she crashed blindly into the two escaping thieves. Like skittles, they all tumbled to the floor, Suzanna screaming and thrashing about on top of the mass of bodies.

Jez was up and over in a second, kicking the dropped bat across the floor and well out of reach. Now he had a problem. If he lifted Suzanna off, he'd risk them both being hurt. Instead, Jez jumped heavily onto the chest of the uppermost youth. It was

in this position that the police discovered them. Two of the police officers handcuffed the winded thieves, then led them away. It was all over.

Trembling, Jez leaned over, clutching his side. He had hurt his ribs again and was sure he was going to be sick all over the floor. The woman was crying, so was Suzanna. She was clutching his leg and whimpering.

"Come on, Suzie," Jez cajoled. "Let's get mum's bread."

"Not so quick, you two," a burly policeman stated, blocking out the sunlight in front of Jez. "You were very foolish, trying to stop those thieves. You could have been hurt. You should have known better, lad. Your little sister is terrified."

Jez sighed. He would never win.

"I'll need your names please," the policeman continued, a touch more kindly. "We'll need to get your description of what happened," he added, flicking open his little black book.

Jez did the necessary, struggling all the while to keep a tight hold of his sister. She wanted to go home.

They were interrupted by the shop assistant. "You leave those kids alone! They were terrific. You have as many sweets as you like. Here, I'll get you a bag."

That did it. Jez could no longer hold on to his squirming sister. She'd get her sweets after all, along with lots of other goodies. What would his mum say?

Gillian Goddard

Set a thief to catch a thief

Display an illustration of Jez and Suzanna foiling the thieves in the shop.

PSHE and citizenship learning objectives

◆ To face new challenges positively by collecting information, looking for help, making responsible choices, and taking action (1c).

◆ To research, discuss and debate topical issues, problems and events (2a).

◆ To realise the consequences of anti-social and aggressive behaviours, both on individuals and communities (2c).

◆ To understand that there are different kinds of responsibilities, rights and duties at home, at school and in the community, and that these can sometimes conflict with one another (2d).

◆ To explore how the media present information (2k).

◆ To recognise different risks in different situations and then decide how to behave responsibly (3e).

◆ To know where individuals, families and groups can get help and support (4g).

Background notes

This text addresses the topic of intervening when wrong is being done and the dangers of doing so. This serial story is preceded by 'Look before you leap' on page 121 and followed by 'A friend in need' on page 33.

Vocabulary

Thief, criminal, crime, unfair, illegal, duty, citizen.

Discussing the text

◆ Read the whole story with the children then re-read the introduction and opening section, up to *scared him rigid*. What did Suzanna do that was wrong? Why was Jez *resentful*? (Mum didn't ever seem to see when Suzanna was cheating or being unfair.) Ask the children if they have had any occasions when adults have been unfair because they failed to see what was going on. Discuss the feelings that surround those events. (Resentment, a sense of injustice, anger, frustration and so on.)

◆ Re-read the next part of the story, up to the point where the two children have just entered the petrol station shop. Why wasn't Mum keen for Jez to go out on his own? (It wasn't safe to go out alone, he was still unwell.) What did Suzanna do that was naughty here? What could have happened to her if Jez hadn't looked after her? (If the children raise the child abduction issue, allow it, but leave discussion of this for a special theme.) Why is Jez reluctant to have his little sister with him? (He finds her company annoying, she's naughty and he's worried about losing face if his friends see him.) Discuss Jez's response to his sister's presence. How does he show that he does care about her? (By holding her hand as she crosses the road.)

◆ Re-read to the end of the story. Examine the actions of Suzanna and Jez during the raid. How did Jez try to protect his sister? (By pushing her behind him, then later by jumping on the thief rather than trying to pull her off the thieves.)

◆ Point out that Jez was brave in protecting his sister – it wasn't a sense of public duty that caused him to interfere. However, discuss if Jez or Suzanna *should* have taken on the thieves. (No, because they could have got badly hurt.) What could they have done that was safer, but still useful? (Had a good look at the youths so that they could help the police with descriptions.) Establish that the children know what makes something a crime, that it is not just wrong, but illegal – someone is breaking the law. Ask the children: *If you saw a crime happening in the street, what could you do?* (Phone 999 and summon the police, or tell a police officer on the beat, tell a parent or other safe adult, make sure you can describe the criminal.)

◆ Ask the children: *If a friend of yours was breaking the law in some way, what could and should you do?* Brainstorm a range of alternatives, for example *Do nothing, Tell him or her it's wrong and he or she should stop, Tell your parents, Report him or her to the police.* Go through the risks, practicalities and consequences of each action, both good and bad. Let the children vote in a secret ballot about what action they would take.

◆ The police officer in the story tells Jez off for getting involved. Was that fair? What was the police officer's point? (It wasn't safe.) Was the shop assistant right in praising them and rewarding them? Why or why not?

PSHE and citizenship activities

◆ In pairs, ask the children to write down descriptions of each other, then produce a police identikit picture and description of this wanted person.

◆ Ask the children to role-play, in small groups, a scene where they are out in the street, going to football practice, and see a crime being committed. What did they do? What happened?

◆ Ask the children to write a version of the story from Suzanna's point of view as she tells her mother all about the incident. Would she describe her exit from the shop as panic?

◆ Invite a police officer to talk about what to do in the event of being aware of or caught up in a crime. If possible, ask the officer to include reference to the kind of crime children can help with detecting, for example by careful observation.

◆ In pairs, ask the children to create a guide for children of their own age who might witness a crime. What should they do? Advise the children to make sure the suggestions in their guides avoid the chance of any child getting hurt.

◆ Talk about what the children should do if they see someone in school doing something that is not a crime, but is nevertheless wrong, for example being nasty to someone else and upsetting them. Explain that the same rules apply about being a good citizen and that they should tell the person to stop, protect others, report the incident to someone in authority or tell their parents.

◆ As a class, re-enact Jez's story for an assembly. Include advice from the guides for being a good citizen and the information given by the police visitor on how school children can help to prevent or stop crime.

Further literacy ideas

◆ In pairs, ask the children to use a word processor to rewrite a section of the story into play format, with stage directions and a list of characters.

◆ Look at the use of adverbs in the story. Tell the children to find and list as many as they can, then go on to create new sentences using these adverbs.

◆ Ask the children to write a newspaper account of the incident, emphasising Jez and Suzanna's bravery. Remind them to include a headline and a picture.

◆ Look at the way names are often contracted, such as Jez and Suzie. Ask the children to come up with as many examples of contracted names as possible, starting with their own classmates.

Managing money

DATE	DESCRIPTION OF ENTRY	AMOUNT
2/1	Christmas money	£10.00
7/1	part of pocket money	£2.00
14/1	part of pocket money	£2.00
21/1	part of pocket money	£2.00
28/1	part of pocket money	£2.00
11/2	part of pocket money	£2.00
13/2	Birthday money	£2.00
28/2	Money for cleaning Mum's car	£15.00
		£2.50
	Total	£37.50
3/3	Withdrawn for PlayStation game	£35.99
	Balance	£ 1.51

GAMES R US

3.3.02 Till number 4

Dynamo-Rangers II

Due   £35.99

Received   £40.00

Change   £4.01

VAT no. 10235448924593574

Managing money

Display different ways of savings money, such as a piggy bank, a post office savings account book, building society passbook, child bank account paying-in book.

PSHE and citizenship learning objectives

◆ To set personal goals (1b).
◆ To look after their money and realise that future wants and needs may be met through saving (1f).
◆ To be aware of different types of relationship, including those between family and friends, and to develop the skills to be effective in relationships (4c).

Background notes

This text addresses an important aspect of citizenship – that of children understanding the value of money, learning to manage their money and how this will be an integral part of their adult lives. Learning to spend and save sensibly helps children acquire self-control and a sense of responsibility.

Vocabulary

Saving account, receipt, account book, pension.

Discussing the text

◆ Ask the children what this text is about. What story does it tell us? (Someone has saved up their money to buy something.) Ask the children if they think this person saving the money is an adult or a child, or boy or a girl. (It's a child because of reference to pocket money, but the reasons for gender selection would be productive to explore with children. They may suggest a boy because being asked to wash the car and being interested in computer games are 'typical' of boys, but there's no reason it couldn't be a girl.)

◆ Do the children think the child was saving specifically for the game or might he or she have been saving already then looked around for something to buy? (It's most likely to have been a planned save, since as soon as the balance showed enough money available, the game was purchased.) Have the children ever saved up for something special?

◆ Why didn't the child's mum or dad buy this game for him or her? Accept a range of possibilities, for example they couldn't afford it, they didn't want him to have it, they felt he should save up his pocket money for something if he wanted it, he wanted to buy it himself, he wanted to give it as a present to someone else. If the children come up with the gift idea, ask if that amount was reasonable for a friend or relative. (It's probably excessive for a child's gift in relation to this child's income.) Make the point that expensive gifts are not necessary to show friendship and caring or love. It is the thought that counts and the care with which it is chosen or presented, not the amount spent on a present. Remind the children that their parents often prefer a home-made present to a bought one because a lot of effort and thought went into it.

◆ Look at the account in detail. How much pocket money do the children think this child received each week? How much of it is being saved? (Express this as a percentage of the figure suggested.) Look at the dates. Does the boy save some pocket money each week? (No.) Why might that be?

Make the point that saving is something we do regularly, if possible, or when we can. If we save, we can buy expensive things that we want. We have greater choice.

◆ How else does the child acquire money to put into his savings account? (As gifts to him for Christmas and his birthday, and earning it by doing jobs.) Do the children in the class do any jobs to get money? Do any of them think they will try to get a regular part-time job when they are older? What sort of job would they like to have?

◆ Discuss where children can save their money. For example in a piggy bank or a savings account.

◆ Explain that adults save for their old age by putting away a small amount of their earnings throughout their working life so that they can have money to spend when they are no longer earning a wage. Explain that this is usually in the form of a pension.

◆ Ask children if they feel that the amount paid for the game was reasonable. Would they pay that much of their own money for a similar computer game? If not, what would they buy if they have saved some money?

PSHE and citizenship activities

◆ Ask the children to work out an imaginary personal savings plan in order to buy something special. Tell them to think about how they will acquire the money, how long it will take to save up. Remind them that they will need to allow some of the money to be used on personal expenditure each week.

◆ Investigate the different types of children's savings accounts available using the Internet or publicity leaflets. As a whole class, discuss which seems to be the best deal. List the pros and cons of each. Introduce the concept of earning interest and mention the ease of depositing and withdrawing money, minimum deposits and so on. Theft and security are also issues too, if the children think of keeping their money in a piggy bank.

◆ Explore the possibility of the school linking with a bank or building society to run a school savings club to encourage saving. If this isn't practical, you may be able to arrange a visit to a bank or building society branch to look at how things are done.

◆ If appropriate, the children could talk with their parents about how they save money for the future and note down their ideas. This will need to be addressed carefully as some parents are not in a position to save money.

◆ Ask the children in groups of two or three to role-play a scene between parents and a child. Explain that in the scene the child keeps on to his or her mum and dad about wanting an expensive toy that the parents cannot afford to buy. What happens? How do the parents help the child understand the situation?

Further literacy ideas

◆ Together, compile a glossary of financial terms and definitions, for example *account, income, outgoings, receipts, investment, pension*.

◆ Look at the format of account books. Ask the children to design their own accounts page on the computer, allowing for a written summary of the payment in and expenditure. Remind them to label the columns.

◆ Ask the children to find as many words as they can that comply with the rule *i before e except after c when the sound is* e, for example *receipt, receive, deceive, achieve, relief, believe* and *thief*.

◆ Ask the children to imagine that a friend keeps buying them expensive gifts, and they do not have enough money to buy equally expensive gifts in return. Tell them to write a short story about what happens and encourage them to include realistic and properly presented dialogue.